GW01048696

EIGHTIES NEW YORK

Also by Michael George

The Statue of Liberty

The Gardens of Ireland
(Text by Patrick Bowe)

New York Today

The South Downs
Travels Through White Cliff Country
(Foreword by Denis Healey)

The Gardens of Spain
(Text by Consuelo Martínez Correcher)

The South Downs
(Foreword by David Dimbleby)

Sussex by the Sea
(Foreword by Michael York)

Megan George
A Tribute

EIGHTIES NEW YORK
A PORTRAIT IN BLACK AND WHITE

Photographs and Text
by
MICHAEL GEORGE

MONTEREY PRESS

Author's edition limited to 50
each one signed and numbered

Michael George 22/50

First published in 2019 by
Monterey Press

Photographs and text copyright © Michael George 2019

The right of Michael George to be identified as the author of this work
has been asserted by him in accordance with the Copyright, Designs and Patents Act 1988

All rights reserved.
No part of this publication may be reproduced, stored in a retrieval system,
or transmitted, in any form or by any means, electronic, mechanical, photocopying,
recording or otherwise, without prior permission in writing of the copyright holder

This book is sold subject to the condition that it shall not, by way of trade or otherwise,
be lent, resold, hired out, or otherwise circulated without the publisher's prior consent
in any form of binding or cover other than that in which it is published and without a similar
condition including this condition being imposed on the subsequent purchaser

A catalogue record for this book is available from the British Library

ISBN 978-0-9560188-2-3
Printed in Great Britain by Nima Print & Design Services Limited, Eastbourne, East Sussex

This book can be ordered direct from the publisher at the website:
www.montereypress.co.uk

Special thanks to:

Robin Darwall-Smith
Howard Davies
Graham Diprose
Michael Hopkins
Tracey Langford
Matt Mason
Nick Mason
Paul Potter
William Roth
Simon Shuel

Each of the images selected and sequenced by the author for this book
may be found in The Archives, University College, Oxford, under the heading
Photographs and Papers of Michael George (b. 1943)
www.univ.ox.ac.uk/about/archives/

In memory of my mother
Megan George
1916 - 2015

"You will have heard of our taking of New Amsterdam, which lies just by New England. 'Tis a place of great importance to trade. It did belong to England heretofore, but the Dutch by degrees drove people out and built a very good town, but we have got the better of it, and 'tis now called New York."

Charles II, in a letter to his sister Henrietta d'Orléans, 1664

8

9

14

"Wealth is not without its advantages and the case to the contrary, although it has often been made, has never proved widely persuasive."

John Kenneth Galbraith, *The Affluent Society*, 1958

21

29

31

"Photography's central sense of purpose and aesthetic: the precise and lucid description of significant fact."

John Szarkowski, Museum of Modern Art, 1971

35

41

43

47

49

"The less people like America, the more they seem to love New York. What looks like a contradiction is explained away by the claim that New York is 'nothing like' the rest of the States. This widely held theory is particularly popular among America's harshest critics ... According to them, New York is not really in America at all."

Decca Aitkenhead, "The Trouble with New York,"
The Guardian, 9 July 2005

53

54

71

75

"Photography first comes into its own as an extension of the eye of the middle-class *flâneur* ... The photographer is an armed version of the solitary walker reconnoitring, stalking, cruising the urban inferno, the voyeuristic stroller who discovers the city as a landscape of voluptuous extremes."

Susan Sontag, *On Photography*, 1977

85

91

93

"The Park throughout is a single work of art, and as such subject to the primary law of every work of art, namely, that it shall be framed upon a single, noble motive, in which the design of all the parts, in some more or less subtle way, shall be confluent and helpful."

Greensward Plan, submission to the
Board of Commissioners of the Central Park, 1858

104

"Sir, among the anfractuosities of the human mind, I know not if it may be one, that there is a superstitious reluctance to sit for a picture."

Samuel Johnson, *Boswell's Life of Johnson*, 3rd edition 1799

"The camera's presence in the city offends against the urban pact whereby we abide the congestion which has denied us privacy by politely ignoring one another. To be photographed is to be stared at, which urban etiquette forbids ... Thus the photographic act becomes the rudest and (in a city) most perilous of detonations: a pointing of the finger."

Peter Conrad, "The Photographer as Citizen,"
Views and Versions of New York, 1984

135

144

"I sit here of a night surrounded by the lovely trophies of my art, and what have they done for me? Ruined me."

Charles Dickens, *Our Mutual Friend*, 1864

TEXT

[iii] – *Puck*. Puck Building, 295-309 Lafayette Street, SE corner Houston Street, SoHo, Downtown Manhattan. Henry Baerer (1837-1908), sculptor. Albert Wagner, architect. 1885, 1895.

The eponymous *Puck*, by the German-born sculptor Henry Baerer, gleefully poses at the northern corners on Houston Street, and, in gilded form, above the entrance on Lafayette Street, of the playful Puck building, Albert Wagner's adaptation of the *Rundbogenstil*, a German building style. Built in the area where industry flourished in the nineteenth century, the block-square, Romanesque Revival building, with its skilful use of moulded red brick, and its horizontal bands of arched windows, was the largest building in the world devoted to lithography and publishing. From 1887 to 1916, it was home to *Puck*, a humour magazine similar to the British *Punch*. In the same mischief-making spirit represented by the curly-headed, near-naked imp, the Puck Building, in more recent times, has given shelter to the gadfly *Spy*, a monthly magazine, best described, in a published letter to the editor, as "snappy." Among "the usual suspects" to be targeted have been: "Hizzoner" Edward I. Koch, Mayor of the City of New York, 1977-87 ("crazy Eddie"), and a billionaire builder from Queens ("short-fingered vulgarian Donald J. Trump").

SoHo, defined as the 33-block area south of Houston (pronounced "*How*-ston"), bounded by Canal Street, West Broadway, and Lafayette Street, once threatened with destruction as a wasteland of useless, nineteenth-century industrial buildings, was saved by campaigners for the preservation of the world's greatest concentration of cast-iron architecture, and by artists attracted by the possibilities of having affordable studios in enormous lofts with lots of light. In the SoHo Cast-Iron Historic District, designated 14 August 1973, the very latest model on offer of *La Vie Bohème*, inevitably, attracted galleries, boutiques, bars, and restaurants. In the chic and expensive residential and retail area, the Puck Building was the go-to location of some of New York's smartest parties and high-end fashion shoots. And the artists have had to move on, to Hoboken, New Jersey, or to Brooklyn or Long Island.

[v] – Brooklyn Bridge (detail). From Frankfort Street and Park Row (City Hall Park), east across the East River to Brooklyn, Downtown Manhattan. John Augustus Roebling (1806-69), Washington Augustus Roebling (1837-1926), and Emily Warren Roebling (1843-1903), engineers. 1869-83.

The bridge's four huge cables which support the main span, each 5¾ inches in diameter, rest in 4-foot-high, U-shaped saddles below the roofs of the two vast, neo-Gothic, double-arched, stone towers, each of them, at the top, 136 feet by 53 feet. Attached to the cables are vertical suspender wires. The verticals are crossed, in a radiating web of wire, by diagonal stays, which are attached to the towers at a point just below the saddles.

A successful bridge-builder in America, to which he migrated from his native Germany, with the deep belief in his adopted country as a new hope for mankind, John Roebling conceived of the "East River Bridge" in the 1850s. In 1867, the man acknowledged as one of the greatest minds in nineteenth-century America, wrote, in the preface to his Report to the New York Bridge Company:

"The contemplated work, when constructed in accordance with my designs, will not only be the greatest Bridge in existence, but it will be the greatest engineering work of this continent, and of the age. Its most conspicuous features, the great towers, will serve as landmarks to the adjoining cities, and they will be entitled to be ranked as national monuments."

The creator did not live to see his bridge; John Roebling died in 1869 as a result of a cruel accident. Shortly after the approval of his plan, while inspecting a possible site of the Brooklyn Tower, his right foot was crushed against a pier by an incoming ferry, and, although the toes were immediately amputated, gangrene set in, and within weeks, he was dead. He was succeeded as Chief Engineer by his son, Washington Roebling, whom he had involved in the work of building the Cincinnati-Covington Bridge, a suspension bridge over the Ohio River in Kentucky, completed in 1867. Although stricken in the summer of 1872 by "caisson disease" (the bends), a disabling, and, in many cases, fatal disease, which also struck down dozens of the work force, he continued, from a sickbed at his house on Brooklyn Heights, with the indispensable support of his wife Emily, his amanuensis and intermediary, to supervise every detail of the construction. But the bridge remains in all essentials John Roebling's; his plan gave the structure its shape and its reality. His masterpiece, the first bridge of steel, the first bridge over the East River, for the first time, linked the City of New York and the City of Brooklyn (incorporated as a city in 1834). Officially called the New York and Brooklyn Bridge, its name was changed in 1915 to the Brooklyn Bridge, not unreasonably, since Brooklyn paid two-thirds of the $25 million cost.

The two towers of the bridge, each 276 feet 6 inches above high water, were constructed with blocks of New York limestone below the high-water mark and Maine granite above. Only the steeple of Richard Upjohn's 1846 Trinity Church in Downtown Manhattan was higher (only just). Brooklyn Bridge, 1,595 feet 6 inches from tower to tower, total length, including the approaches, 5,989 feet, was the longest suspension bridge in the world. Nothing in nineteenth-century New York caused more excitement, or symbolised America's sense of manifest destiny better, than Brooklyn Bridge, which, as Alan Trachtenbergh has written, "was created in travail amidst corruption" (*Brooklyn Bridge/Fact and Symbol*, 1965). On 24 May 1883, the day of the formal opening, one hundred and fifty thousand people walked across Brooklyn Bridge, among them, leading a ceremonial parade, President of the United States Chester A. Arthur, a New Yorker, accompanied by Governor of New York State, and future President, Grover Cleveland. The President and the Governor were met, on the Brooklyn side, by Emily Roebling, representing her invalid husband. They later went to congratulate Washington Roebling at the Roeblings' home on Brooklyn Heights.

"All modern New York, heroic New York, started with Brooklyn Bridge."

Kenneth Clark, *Civilisation*, 1969

[xi] – Tony Neal, as MC, in a doorway, Far West Village, Downtown Manhattan, May 1980.

[1] – *The Horse Tamers* (detail). Park Circle entrance, Prospect Park, Middle Brooklyn. One of two bronze groups on ornamented granite pedestals. Frederick William MacMonnies (1863-1937), sculptor. Stanford White (1853-1906), architect. 1899.

[2–3] – *America, The Four Continents*. US Custom House, 1 Bowling Green, Battery and Whitehall District, Downtown Manhattan. Marble groups; granite pedestals. Daniel Chester French (1850-1931), sculptor. Cass Gilbert (1859-1934), architect. 1907.

Overlooking Bowling Green, probably New York's first public park, the US Custom House is one of the most beautiful and impressive of Beaux-Arts buildings: Cass Gilbert's granite palace, with four massive Corinthian columns, was built to signify the importance of New York as a great seaport, receiving goods from the four corners of the globe. The four continents, America, Europe, Asia, and Africa, which grace the building, are depicted as seated women. America is the most vigorously modelled: "Her head raised and in her eyes there is a look of one seeing a vision." In her right hand she holds the torch of liberty, while her left arm shields the kneeling figure of a young man with a winged wheel signifying "the inventive genius of modern America and her industrial enterprise." In her lap are stalks of corn. A Native American crouches behind.

[4–5] – Skylines

(*left*) A view toward the north-east from the Empire State Building, Midtown Manhattan, of:

Chrysler Building, 405 Lexington Avenue, NE corner 42nd Street. William Van Alen (1883-1945), architect. 1930.

Van Alen had originally designed it as a speculative office building, but Walter P. Chrysler, looking for a headquarters in New York for the corporation that bears his name, bought the lease on the property, and asked the architect for a distinctive tower. Even though it long ago changed hands, the building will always be linked with the golden age of motoring. Presumably, Chrysler asked for the automobile icons: the winged Mercury radiator caps, and the frieze of hubcaps and mudguards, among them. The sleek, mirrorlike quality of stainless steel made it a favourite Art Deco building material, even though it was exorbitantly expensive. The 77-storey tower is topped by six levels of stainless steel wrapping triangular windows. Van Alen was neck-and-neck with his great rival H. Craig Severance, the architect of 40 Wall Street, in Downtown Manhattan. At the last minute, he bolted into position, above the radiant arches, a secret spire, thereby snatching the title of world's tallest building, at 1,048 feet, 64 feet taller than the Eiffel Tower.

and

Pan Am Building (from 1981, MetLife Building), 200 Park Avenue, between 44th and 45th streets. Emery Roth & Sons, architects. Walter Gropius (The Architects' Collaborative) and Pietro Belluschi, design consultants. 1963.

In the vertical city, the erection, over some of Grand Central Terminal's air rights, on a 3.5-acre site, of a 59-storey, precast concrete, octagonal tower, providing 2.4 million square feet of rentable office space, was universally condemned:

"What is lacking is any sense of scale, any sense of grace … shouldering aside all sense of proportion and elegance in its gigantism."

John Tauranac, *Essential New York/A Guide to the History and Architecture of Manhattan's Important Buildings, Parks, and Bridges*, 1979

"the precast concrete monster … this act of destruction of the cityscape … the epitome of irresponsible planning and design … an arrogant, oversize intruder."

Paul Goldberger, *The City Observed: New York/ A Guide to the Architecture of Manhattan*, 1979

(*right*) A view north toward Midtown from the roof of the Braveman Building, 2 East Broadway, NE corner Catherine Street, Chinatown, Downtown Manhattan.

The ornate, neoclassical building with a stately dome, foreground, was designed in 1894 by Stanford White (1853-1906), of the prestigious, Beaux-Arts-trained architects McKim, Mead & White, for the Bowery Savings Bank (now Home Savings of America). The building at 130 Bowery, NW corner Grand Street, in the words of Paul Goldberger, "on the Bowery amidst winos and junkies … is a staggering presence" (*The City Observed: New York/A Guide to the Architecture of Manhattan*, 1979).

By contrast, the Midtown skyline offers, in the words of the gallery owner, photographer, and avant-garde leader Alfred Stieglitz, "America without that damned French flavor!" Two Art Deco masterpieces, the quintessential New York skyscrapers, are, *right*, with the shiny-steel, needle-like spire, the Chrysler Building (1930), and, *left*, its superb main shaft of limestone and steel rising in an almost unbroken line, the Empire State building (1931).

New York lagged behind Chicago in building the first skyscraper, "defined as a building supported by a steel skeleton construction with walls that did not bear the load" (John Tauranac, *Essential New York/A Guide to the History and Architecture of Manhattan's Important Buildings, Parks, and Bridges*, 1979). The race was on during the 1920s for The Tallest Building In The World, and the clear winner, at 1,472 feet, including the slender TV antenna, was the Empire State Building, 350 Fifth Avenue, between 33rd and 34th streets (Shreve, Lamb & Harmon, architects. 1931). Having taken the title from the Chrysler Building, completed less than a year earlier, it lost out to the World Trade Center in the 1970s. When the Empire State Building was opened, space was so difficult to rent that it was nicknamed "the Empty Building," and only the immediate popularity of the observatories saved it from bankruptcy. The architectural importance of the structure far transcends the matter of height alone. A monument to an epoch, the boom years from 1924 to 1929, the Empire State Building is a symbol of the power of the great Eastern megalopolis.

The 86th floor observatory, 1,050 feet up, was the venue of the launch party, 12 October 1986, hosted by Harry N. Abrams, Inc., Publishers, New York, and Olympus Corporation, for the photographer's first book on the city, *New York Today*.

[6–7] – A view of Downtown Manhattan from the north.

(*left*) At the southern tip of Manhattan Island an assembly of monoliths, seemingly devoid of people, presents itself. Here, in the oldest part of the city, as nowhere else, are many unexpected juxtapositions: Colonial-era structures cheek by jowl with twentieth-century skyscrapers. Emerging from the deep shadow cast by the encroaching towers of the Financial District (*lower right*) is St Paul's Chapel, between Broadway, Fulton, Church, and Vesey streets (Thomas McBean, architect. 1764-66; steeple, James Crommelin Lawrence, 1794). New York's premier Georgian church was built on Broadway (from the Dutch *Brede Wegh*), and, uniquely, with its back to Broadway, the major North-South thoroughfare which began as an Indian trail known as the Weekquaesyeek. A chapel-of-ease, or dependency, of Trinity Church, at the time a church built entirely of wood, to the south, St Paul's, was built on land that was part of Trinity's extensive holdings that spread north to Greenwich Village, in a field sloping to the Hudson River. Constructed with stone quarried on site, the Manhattan schist on which many of New York's skyscrapers stand, St Paul's, a rectangular edifice with an Ionic portico, reckoned to be the grandest church in America, reflects the influence of St Martin-in-the-Fields in London. McBean, a Scot, was a pupil of James Gibbs, the architect of the rectangular edifice with a portico, 1722-24, that stands at the northeastern corner of Trafalgar Square. It was to St Paul's Chapel, New York's only pre-Revolutionary church, that George Washington came, accompanied by both houses of Congress, immediately following his taking the oath of office as first President of the United States of America, 30 April 1789. Washington, who lived in the Executive Mansion at 39 Broadway when New York was the nation's capital, continued to worship at St Paul's. His pew is maintained under the Great Seal of the United States.

"As the sky grew to epic proportions, New York became known as the unbelievable city."

Susan Lubowsky, *Precisionist Perspectives/Prints and Drawings*, Whitney Museum of American Art at Philip Morris, 120 Park Avenue, New York, NY 10017, 2 March-28 April 1988. Catalogue, collection the photographer

(*right*) A view south toward Downtown Manhattan from the Empire State Building.

The tight little island of Manhattan is 12½ miles at its longest and 2½ at its widest. One cannot look in any direction in Manhattan without seeing water at the end of the street: the Hudson and East Rivers, Upper New York Bay. A City Commission in 1811 imposed on much of the island a grid-iron plan of right-angled streets and avenues, with Fifth Avenue, seen here, dividing the cross-town streets into east and west. New York's oldest and longest street, Broadway, which has always been the city's spine, intersects with Fifth Avenue at 23rd Street, at which meeting point, in 1902, Chicago architect Daniel Burnham built his masterpiece, the Flatiron Building, once New York's most famous skyscraper. Due south of the Empire State Building, Fifth Avenue, NW corner 34th Street, at a distance of one and a half miles, is Washington Arch, at the northern edge of Washington Square, where Fifth Avenue has its beginning. The granite arch, 77 feet high, 62 feet wide, designed by Stanford White, is where George Washington greeted his troops after the evacuation of the British army of occupation. The present arch, of 1895, replaced an earlier wooden one, built in 1889 to commemorate the centennial of Washington's taking the oath of office as first President of the United States. At the southern tip of Manhattan Island, outlined against the waters of Upper New York Bay, and half-hidden in haze, is a huddled mass of towers, among them the Twin Towers of the World Trade Center. Here, at the turn of the twentieth century, skyscrapers multiplied rapidly. To describe the scene, the word "skyline" appeared. Building was halted by the Great Crash of 1929. A postwar boom followed. Now, Downtown Manhattan, from the Battery to 14th Street, a solid wall of structures extends, almost unbroken.

"An almost Nietzschean individualism, the kind symbolized by the great skyscrapers in the bright sky of New York."

Jean-Paul Sartre, "Individualism and Conformism," 1945

[8–9] – Municipal Building, 1 Centre Street, at Chambers Street, Downtown Manhattan. William Mitchell Kendall (1856-1941), senior partner, McKim, Mead & White, architects. 1909-13.

At the beginning of the twentieth century, the Beaux-Arts-trained architects McKim, Mead & White were the most prestigious in New York. Not having built a skyscraper before, they took on the challenge of building on an awkward site offices for the bureaucracy of city government, which had recently consolidated all five boroughs of Greater New York City, the neighbourhoods of ethnic origin that are small cities in themselves. William Mitchell Kendall designed, 1907-08, a massive, flattened U-shape of a building straddling Chambers Street, comprised of a 25-storey "base" and "shaft," classically inspired and restrained in treatment, and a 10-storey, baroque mélange of colonnades, balustrades, urns, obelisks, and pyramidal domes, surmounted by Adolph Alexander Weinman's *Civic Fame*, a 25-foot-high, gilded copper sculpture of a classically robed female figure, her head encircled by a garland of laurel, the emblem of victory, and, in her extended left hand, holding a turret-shaped crown. This wedding cake sequence fronts:

(*left*) One and Two World Trade Center (North Tower and South Tower), between Church, Vesey, West, and Liberty streets, Downtown Manhattan. Minoru Yamasaki & Associates; Emery Roth & Sons, architects. 1966-73.

More than 1.2 million cubic yards of earth and rock were excavated to make way for the Trade Center, built by the Port Authority of New York and New Jersey on a 16-acre site in Downtown Manhattan. (Placed in the Hudson River, the excavated material, 23.5 acres of landfill, deeded to the City of New York, were developed as Battery Park City.)

The Twin Towers, 1,350 feet of sheer uninterrupted steel and glass, two 110-storey rectilinear buildings, each over 200 by 200 square feet, and separated from each other by a distance of 130 feet, provided over 7.9 million square feet of rentable office space. An estimated 1.5 million visitors a year were drawn by the promise of spectacular views from the Observation Deck at Two World Trade Center.

On 11 September 2001 (9/11) global jihadi strikes on New York and Washington DC – 15 of the 19 hijackers of US passenger planes were Saudis – killed 2,976 and injured more than 6,000, totally destroying the Twin Towers, the tallest building in New York and the second tallest in the world.

(*right*) US Courthouse, 40 Centre Street, between Duane and Pearl streets, Downtown Manhattan. Cass Gilbert (1859-1934); Cass Gilbert Jr, architects. 1936.

A lanthorn caps the gilt pyramidal roof, part of which is seen here, that crowns the 25-storey tower that bursts, not entirely convincingly, from a neoclassical temple base, with a grandiose Corinthian portico, approached from Foley Square by a broad flight of granite steps. Cass Gilbert, the architect of the nearby Woolworth Building, his Gothic Revival masterpiece of 1913, began to design this federal courthouse a year before his death in 1934; it was completed by his son Cass Gilbert Jr two years later.

[10–11] – *The Spirit of Communication* ("Golden Boy"). American Telephone and Telegraph Building, 195 Broadway between Fulton and Dey streets, Downtown Manhattan. (*left*) Park Row Building, 15 Park Row, between Beekman and Ann streets (R. H. Robertson, architect. 1899). (*right*) South Tower, World Trade Center. In the late nineteenth and early twentieth centuries "Newspaper Row" was situated on Park Row. The 91-storey Park Row Building was one of the tallest buildings in the world at the date of its completion. Resting on a massive body of structural steel, faced with brick, stone, and glass, are twin domed towers, each topped with a Baroque-style cupola articulated by piers decorated with female heads. The heads have been attributed to the sculptor J. Massey Rhind. R. H. Robertson was one of the many leading New York architects at the turn of the century working within the Beaux-Arts tradition of architectural decoration imported into America from Paris.

John Massey Rhind (1860-1936) was born in Edinburgh. A third-generation sculptor who came to America after being trained in London and Paris, he was best known for his public monuments and architectural sculpture.

A 24-foot-tall, gilt bronze, winged nude male figure, on a globe, also gilt, holds in his raised left hand bolts of lightning and, in his right, cabling, which also coils about his torso. He stands atop a stepped pyramidal concrete structure, carried by a square, colonnaded temple (Evelyn Beatrice Longman, sculptor. 1915. William Welles Bosworth, architect. 1917).

Created for the headquarters of American Telephone and Telegraph, a building said to have more columns than any other building in the world, Evelyn Beatrice Longman's gilt, bronze sculpture was, for more than half a century, the corporate symbol of AT&T. The decision to remove it, in 1980, stirred conservationists to object that such a splendid element of the Financial District's skyline should be maintained. When the statue was encased in scaffolding, and then, again, on the day of its being dismantled, the photographer, without benefit of insurance or hard hat, was granted by the corporation unique access to photograph Golden Boy up close and personal.

It is said that when AT&T suggested to the restorer that something might be done to disguise "Boy's" obviously "boyish" attributes, she responded: "I will gild; I will not geld." So, *The Spirit of Communication Redivivus* was given pride of place in the vaulted main lobby of the AT&T Building on Madison Avenue, between 55th and 56th streets (Johnson & Burgee, architects), the hugely controversial, postmodern, 37-storey tower with an immense broken pediment at top, frequently compared to a Chippendale highboy, completed 15 August 1983. Within a surprisingly short space of time, AT&T bailed out of their OTT quarters taking their oversize mascot with them to suburban New Jersey.

and

(*right*) *Liberty Enlightening the World* (Statue of Liberty). Liberty (former Bedloe's) Island, Upper New York Bay. Sculpture comprised of 300 repoussé copper plates, each 3/32 of an inch thick, attached to an intricate iron and steel frame, 151 feet high and weighing 225 tons, on a pedestal of granite blocks and concrete, 89 feet high, set within the angular bastions of the star-shaped Fort Wood (1808-11). Frédéric Auguste Bartholdi (1834-1904), sculptor. Alexandre Gustave Eiffel (1834-1932), engineer. Richard Morris Hunt (1827-95), architect. 1886.

Bartholdi portrayed Liberty as a woman stepping from broken shackles. In her uplifted right hand she holds a flaming torch, while in her left she holds a tablet representing the Declaration of Independence, inscribed "JULY IV MDCCLXXVI." The seven rays of her crown represent the seven seas and seven continents. Conceived of as standing at the gateway to the New World, the colossus, on its island at the entrance to the harbour, is outlined against the great mouth of the Hudson River. A gift of the French people to commemorate "the alliance of the two nations in achieving the independence of the United States of America," Lady Liberty attests their abiding friendship. The statue was shipped in 214 cases aboard the French ship *Isère* in May 1885. President Grover Cleveland dedicated the monument on 28 October 1886. In a much-needed, major, year-long restoration in 1985, costing $69.8 million, a new torch, its flame coated in 24-carat gold, replaced the corroded original. Amid city-wide celebrations, the torch was "relit" by President Ronald W. Reagan, 3 July 1986.

The photographer, whose first book, in 1985, was *The Statue of Liberty*, published by Harry N. Abrams, Inc., in 1986, was invited by the US Navy to be one of the official team of photographers assigned to photograph events for a limited edition, commemorative volume, with Remarks by President Reagan, *The Liberty Centennial 1886-1986: The Fourth of July Weekend.*

[12] – *Giovanni da Verrazano* (detail). Battery Park, Downtown Manhattan. Bronze bust; granite pedestal. Ettore Ximenes (1855-1926), sculptor. The monument was a gift from New York's Italian community, 1909.

A Florentine navigator, in the employ of France, Giovanni da Verrazano (1485-1528), was the first white man to see the southern tip of Manhattan Island. He led an expedition in 1524 that explored New York Bay and the coastline as far north as Cape Breton in Canada. Four years later he was killed by cannibals in the Caribbean. His name lives on with the Verrazano-Narrows Bridge, linking Brooklyn and Staten Island. Below the bust is a bronze female figure representing *Discovery*. At her feet lies a book symbolising history. Originally, she held a torch in her left hand and a sword in her right hand, both now missing. Ximenes, born in Palermo, studied sculpture against his father's wishes, and sold his first sculpture when he was sixteen.

[13] – *East Coast Memorial* (detail). Battery Park, Downtown Manhattan. Bronze eagle; granite pedestal. Albino Manca, sculptor. William Gehron and Gilbert Seltzer, architects. 1960.

The enormous, stylised bronze eagle is flanked by two rows of four granite slabs, each one inscribed with the names of the over 4,000 Americans whose lives were lost in the coastal waters of the North Atlantic in World War II.

> "I wish the bald eagle had not been chosen as the representative of the country; he is a bird of a bad moral character … The turkey … is a much more respectable bird, and withal a true original native of America."
>
> Benjamin Franklin, Letter to Sarah Bache, 26 January 1784

[14–15] – *George Washington* (details). Federal Hall National Memorial (former Subtreasury Building), Wall and Broad streets, Financial District, Downtown Manhattan. Bronze sculpture; granite pedestal. John Quincy Adams Ward (1830-1910), sculptor. 1883.

(*left*) Washington, his right hand on the Bible, took the oath of office when he was inaugurated as first President, 30 April 1789, standing on the balcony of the original Federal Hall occupying this site, from the steps of which the Declaration of Independence had been read to New Yorkers in 1776, and which was to serve as the first seat of government of the United States. The actual stone on which Washington stood during that historic ceremony is preserved in a glass case within the building. For accuracy in his work, Ward referred to portraits of Washington by Gilbert Stuart and Jean-Antoine Houdon.

(*right*) *Integrity Protecting the Works of Man*. New York Stock Exchange, 8 Broad Street, SW corner Wall Street, Financial District, Downtown Manhattan. Sculptural pediment by John Quincy Adams Ward (1830-1910), sculptor; figures modelled by Paul W. Bartlett. George B. Post, architect. 1903.

From the steps of Federal Hall National Memorial on Wall Street, John Q. A. Ward's *George Washington* of 1883 looks out toward another work created by the sculptor: the sculptural pediment of the 17-storey New York Stock Exchange on Broad Street, built in 1903. The hub of the world's financial markets, the New York Stock

Exchange has the façade of a neoclassical temple, comprising six 52½-foot-high Corinthian pillars, flanked by Corinthian pilasters, with a pediment in which sculptured figures, of heroic proportions, carved out of French limestone, represent Commerce and Industry, and, at the centre, an 18-foot-high statue of Integrity. By 1938 the badly weathered sculptures had deteriorated to the point at which it was determined that they posed a real threat to public safety. In conditions of utmost secrecy, faithful copies were made of lead-coated copper, covered with weather-resistant paint to simulate the limestone, then substituted for the originals, which were taken away and destroyed. The truth was revealed eighteen years later, in 1954, by veteran *New York Times* reporter Meyer ("Mike") Berger.

[16–17] – Appellate Division, New York State Supreme Court Madison Avenue, NE corner 25th Street, Midtown Manhattan. James Brown Lord, architect. 1900.

Sculpture is integral to the design of this magnificent Beaux-Arts marble palace in miniature, which is graced by some of the finest sculpture in the city.

(*left*) *Peace*, flanked by *Wisdom* and *Strength*. Marble group. Karl Bitter (1867-1915), sculptor; and, *right*, *Moses*, marble sculpture. William Couper, sculptor; both 1899.

A view from Madison Square of the frozen white neoclassical figures that unexpectedly enliven the skyline.

Karl Bitter, born in Vienna, came to the United States when he was twenty-one. His work for a firm that executed architectural decoration brought him to the attention of the distinguished architect Richard Morris Hunt, who commissioned him to create ornament for some of America's finest houses and churches. He contributed to the sculptural programmes of several World's Fairs, including the Columbian Exposition at Chicago in 1892. Bitter's best-known work was also to be his last: the lovely statue of *Pomona*, the goddess of abundance, the Pulitzer Memorial Fountain, Grand Army Plaza.

(*right*) *Wisdom*, 29th Street entrance. Marble sculpture on pedestal. Frederick Wellington Ruckstuhl (1853-1942), sculptor.

For the steps leading up to the entrance – a hexastyle crowned by a pediment featuring a group representing *The Triumph of the Law* – Ruckstuhl, a guardian of traditional sculpture in the 1890s, sculpted two seated figures that emphasise the classical balance of the building and represent an abstraction of the scales of justice: the dynamic *Force* and, seen here, the contemplative *Wisdom* (reminiscent of Michelangelo's *Moses*).

Inscription:

EVERY LAW NOT BASED ON WISDOM IS A MENACE TO THE STATE

"Sculpture in public places infuses magic into city life. These stirring images, silent companions in parks and plazas, are symbols of our spirit and past ideals, given permanence in bronze and stone."

Phyllis Samitz Cohen, *Adopt-A-Monument*, The Municipal Art Society
of New York, 1987

[19] – Mrs Vincent (Brooke) Astor (1902-2007), at a party to honour Ashton Hawkins, Executive Vice-President and Counsel to the Trustees, The Metropolitan Museum of Art, Greene Street, SoHo, Downtown Manhattan, May 1987.

Philanthropist, socialite, writer, and chairwoman of the Vincent Astor Foundation, Roberta Brooke Russell Astor, known as Bobby to close friends and family, was the unofficial first lady of New York. Married first, at the age of sixteen, to millionaire distillery buff J. Dryden Kuser, Brooke then married the investor Charles H. ("Buddie") Marshall. Following his death in 1952, she then married, in 1953, Vincent Astor, son of John Jacob Astor IV and great-great-grandson of America's first multimillionaire, John Jacob Astor. On the death of Vincent Astor in 1979, Brooke inherited outright $2 million; about $65 million in investments; and, most importantly, control of the Vincent Astor Foundation, her late husband's personal foundation, established in 1948, the $67 million in assets of which were to be used "for the alleviation of human misery." A committed New Yorker, Brooke Astor said that her Foundation was her life. She is credited with having saved New York Public Library; supporting projects in the Bronx and Bedford-Stuyvesant, two of the city's most deprived areas; and giving $18 million to the Metropolitan Museum of Art. It has been estimated that, in gifts and investments, she gave New York, over a 25-year period, a staggering $130 million. In the process, as Brooke Astor observed, she made herself "the *nouveau pauvre*, compared to others" (Julie Baumgold, "The Joy of Giving," "The Style of New York," *New York*, Year-End Double Issue, 24-31 December 1984).

[20–23] – A party for newly-wed Barbara Walters and Merv Adelson given by Mrs Vincent (Brooke) Astor and Mrs Gordon P. (Ann) Getty. The Astor Court, The Metropolitan Museum of Art, Fifth Avenue, west side, 80th to 84th streets, Upper East Side, Uptown Manhattan, 20 October 1986.

(**20**, *above*) Veteran TV broadcaster Barbara Walters, 54, and her husband Merv Adelson, head of Lorimar Telepictures, greet friends in the glittering world of money, power, and celebrity, at the bash for *le tout New York*. Ms Walters put a crack in the glass ceiling, 4 October 1976, when she became co-anchor of Harry Reasoner on ABC Television at $1 million a year.

(**20**, *below*) HIM Empress Farah, the former Persian Empress and the last Queen of Iran, makes an entrance, having first shed her Iranian personal protection officer. Her Imperial Majesty wears a statement necklace of emeralds, diamonds, and pearls, and matching drop earrings. Born, the daughter of an army officer, in Tehran in 1938, Farah Diba was a student of architecture in Paris before her marriage, as his third wife, to Mohammad Reza Shah Pahlavi, in Tehran, in December 1959. The Shah had been installed in power six years earlier, in August

1953, in a coup covertly organised by MI6 and the CIA, which overthrew Iran's popular, nationalist government under Mohammad Mossadegh. "The Shah subsequently used widespread repression and torture to institute a dictatorship that lasted until the 1979 Islamic revolution" (Mark Curtis, *Web of Deceit/Britain's Real Role in the World*, 2003). At the Golestan Palace, Tehran, 26 October 1967, the Shah, seated on the fabled, gem-encrusted Peacock Throne, crowned himself Aryamehr Shahanshah – Light of the Aryans and King of Kings – and placed a crown on the head of his wife Farah, the first Shahbanou, or Empress, formally crowned since seventh-century Arabs defeated the Persians and introduced Islam.

(**21**) Malcolm Forbes (1919-90). The publisher of the business magazine that bears his name, the self-styled "capitalist tool," and propagandist-in-chief of the winner-takes-all financial model, Forbes was the ever-smiling frequenter of celebrity circles. The hot-air balloonist, black-biker-leather-clad motorcyclist, was also the collector *extraordinaire* of toy soldiers and Fabergé jewelled eggs. In August 1989, to celebrate his seventieth birthday, he invited eight hundred of his most intimate friends, among them Elizabeth Taylor, whom he was said to be romancing, to a $2 million "party of the century" at his palace, the Palais Madoub, in Tangier, Morocco. Within six months, the high-profile party-giver was dead of a heart attack at Timberfield, his estate in Far Hills, New Jersey.

"There is one and only one social responsibility of business … to increase its profits."

Milton Friedman

(**22**, *above*) (*left to right*) Merv Adelson, Bill Blass, Lynn Wyatt, and Gayfryd Steinberg.

Houston grande dame Lynn Wyatt, possessor of a new ranch in South Texas, where husband Oscar has installed an airstrip for his 747, wears her platinum-blonde hair pulled back into a *catogan* with a black grosgrain bow. With her, gauging the temperature of the A-lister-filled room, is top American fashion designer Bill Blass (1922-2002), without whom New York fashion would be "impossible to imagine" (*Town & Country*, September 1987). In 1999 he sold Bill Blass Limited for $50 million, and, in his will, he bequeathed half of his $52 million estate, as well as several important ancient sculptures in his collection, to the Metropolitan Museum of Art. Distinguished by her gelled black DA, Canadian-born Gayfryd Steinberg "grew up in a rented house in Vancouver, British Columbia, the daughter of a telephone company clerk" (Nell Scovell, "How to Marry a Millionaire," headlined "Golddiggers of 1987," *Spy*, September 1987). A former Louisiana businesswoman who ran her own steel pipe business, Gayfryd converted to Judaism on her third marriage to mega-rich Reliance Insurance tycoon Saul Steinberg, also twice divorced. Their art-filled, thirty-room triplex apartment on Park Avenue used to belong to John D. Rockefeller. A Trustee of the New York Public Library, Gayfryd Steinberg married, in 2014, Michael Shnayerson. As editor of *Avenue*, he published, as covers, a number of the photographer's images in colour of New York. As "our new hire," at *Vanity Fair*, contributing editor Michael was asked by editor Tina Brown to contribute a piece "on the toll of AIDS on the arts and fashion," which she ran in the March 1987 issue, with, controversially, "a gallery of faces of all those who have died and denuded us of their talent … in a haunting double-page spread" (Tina Brown, *The Vanity Fair Diaries 1983-1992*, 2017). The first cases of AIDS were diagnosed in 1981.

(**22**, *below*) Mrs William F. (Pat) Buckley Jr (1926-2006). As chairwoman of the Met's Costume Institute gala, from 1978 to 1993, Pat Buckley succeeded in turning it into one of the most prestigious events of the season and helped raise millions of dollars for the museum. Pat Buckley was married to ultra-conservative commentator, William F. Buckley Jr (1925-2008), writer of a nationally syndicated newspaper column; founder, in 1955, of the political journal *National Review*; and host, from 1966 to 1999, of the television show *Firing Line*.

"All conservatives are such from personal defects …"

Ralph Waldo Emerson

[23] – America's "golden couple," Mr and Mrs Donald J. Trump, formidable socialites, were among the glitterati who put in an appearance at the blockbusting bash at the Met.

"The Donald," son of successful Queens real estate developer Fred Trump (ancestral German name, Drumpf) and his Scottish wife, Mary Ann MacLeod, started making real estate deals fresh out of college. At the age of twenty-seven he persuaded the City to scrap property taxes for the next forty years and put up funds for him to develop "run down areas," among them 42nd Street, between Lexington and Vanderbilt avenues, where a sleek new Grand Hyatt Hotel sprang up in place of the tired old Commodore Hotel (which had put up the photographer on his first, *free*, visit to New York, one weekend in October 1970). He went on to amass great wealth, which he showed off by travelling in airplanes, helicopters, yachts, and a stretch Cadillac limo with his name emblazoned on their sides. The real estate tycoon, who came to symbolise the yuppie wealth of the 1980s, and who once said, "Somewhere down the line, I'm not going to have anything to buy," completed Trump Tower on Fifth Avenue in 1983, the year of the economic boom which saw property prices soar. As soon as he bought a property he would turn its management over to the other member of "Team Trump," his wife Ivana, the Czech-born, former Olympic skier and top model, mother of his three children, Ivanka, Donald Jr, and Eric, and chairman of the landmark Plaza Hotel in New York, one of her husband's most recent and more successful acquisitions. When the news broke in 1990 that the Trumps were heading for divorce, Ivana Trump let it be known through her lawyers that she would be looking for a larger share of Donald Trump's fortune, estimated at $1.7 billion, than was spelled out in a prenuptial agreement that was considered "unconscionable and fraudulent." Her demands included: $93 million in cash, a Boeing 727 private jetliner, and the Plaza Hotel – "a fairer payoff for 13 years of hard work, as a wife, mother, hostess and manager of several of Trump's business concerns … some say that it was the admiration of her husband for pretty women that drove Ivana, 42, to keep young and attractive for him. And Ivana herself has no qualms in admitting – as she did in one of several interviews with *Hello!* – that she had actually promised Trump she 'would never age over 28' " ("Donald and Ivana: The Couple Who Lived the American Dream," *Hello!*, 24 February 1990).

"To live in New York in the spring of 1988 is to confront extremes of wealth and poverty unknown since the Gilded Age. Never has the city seemed so full of creativity and energy – and yet so distracted and frivolous. And never in the postwar years have New Yorkers been so conscious of sharing their lives with society's deprived, desperate, and doomed."

Edward Kosner, Editor and Publisher, "How We Live Now," *New York*,
20th Anniversary Special Issue – III, 18 April 1988

[24] – "CRIME IN CHELSEA," a notice in a shop window, Ninth Avenue, Chelsea, Midtown Manhattan. A sign of the times, in which a local community has to come together to tackle the increase in crime in the area.

[25] – "FUCK U.S. CAPITALISM," political messaging, sprayed on a retaining wall, Union Square Park, Midtown Manhattan. The traditional centre of America's radical movement, and the forum for mass protest, Union Square got its name, in 1807, as the meeting place, or union, of Bowery Road and Broadway, then New York's main highway. It was here, 25 November 1786, to be remembered as Evacuation Day, that deliriously happy crowds greeted General George Washington as he entered New York City at the end of the seven-year occupation by British forces during the Revolution. The bronze equestrian sculpture, *George Washington* (14-foot-high granite pedestal; Henry Kirke Brown (1814-86), sculptor, with John Quincy Adams Ward (1802-78); Richard Upjohn (1802-78), architect), commissioned by New York businessmen, was unveiled on the eightieth anniversary of the nation's independence, 4 July 1856. One of the earliest equestrian statues in America, Brown's image of Washington, bare-headed, right arm extended in a gesture of command, and left hand guiding his charger, was clearly inspired by the magnificent classical bronze statue of *Marcus Aurelius* (AD 161-180), in the Piazza del Campidoglio in Rome, a bringer of peace rather than a military hero. In its original location in the middle of the street at Union Square, the monument "fell victim to the chemical and social environment," and although relocated to the position seen here, in Union Square's three-acre park, was in need of complete renovation, at a cost of $28,750, according to *Adopt-A-Monument* (The Municipal Art Society of New York, 1987). Union Square Park, by the 1970s, had deteriorated so badly as to be a no-go area, the haunt of drug-dealers and muggers. On the initiative of local retailers and residents, funds were raised for the restoration and renovation of the park, at a cost of $3.6 million. It was reopened in May 1985.

[26–27] – The Bowery, Downtown Manhattan.

Six farms, or "bouweries," were laid out by the Dutch West India Company in 1628 on the present East Side below 14th Street. No. I was the "Great Bouwerie," later to be the home of Petrus ("Peg-leg Peter") Stuyvesant, Director-General, Nieuw Amsterdam. The Bowery, which later formed part of the highroad to Boston, was originally an Indian trail. After a chequered history, the street went into a seemingly irreversible decline, given over to pawnshops, restaurant equipment houses, beer saloons, and flophouses, in which, at the cost of twenty-five cents for the night, a bug-infested bed could be procured by any one of a growing army of displaced and desperate men drawn from the unemployed around the United States.

(*left*) A young storehand returns to work at M&D Shapiro Hardware Co. Inc., 320 Bowery.

(*right*) An old derelict is doomed to wander the mean streets.

> "In this republican country, amid the fluctuating waves of our social life, somebody is always at the drowning point."
>
> Nathaniel Hawthorne, *The House of Seven Gables*, 1851

[28–29] – Billboards, Lower East Side, Downtown Manhattan.

The garish proliferation of advertising into every corner of the American environment is in evidence in even the poorest quarter of New York City, as here.

(*left*) A young Chinese-American passes an image of a young Latina beaming in a Spanish-language translation the universal consumerist message from a blank-windowed, vacant dwelling on Madison Street at Market Street.

(*right*) A neighbourhood cop stops to look as a young man does a paint job on the wall of a used-car lot on Division Street.

> "From the beginning the settlement which was to become New York City was a commercial enterprise; business is the oldest New York tradition."
>
> Jerry E. Patterson, Foreword by Louis Auchincloss, Introduction by Joseph Veach Noble, *The City of New York/A History Illustrated from the Collections of The Museum of the City of New York*, 1978

[30] – A view from the elevated walkway of Williamsburg Bridge of Pitt Street, between Delancey and Rivington streets, Lower East Side, Downtown Manhattan.

The building of the Williamsburg and Manhattan bridges, 1903 and 1909, cut swathes through the Lower East Side, bringing some light and air to the teeming tenements in unlovely, overcrowded areas of extreme poverty.

[31] – FOUR STEPS RESTAURANT, Downtown Manhattan.

The corner coffee shop, a cherished New York institution, is here housed in a cast-iron building that is showing signs of age. The neighbourhood coffee shop, typically, with plastic flowers in the window, vinyl-covered seats, and Formica tables and counter, is the kind of place where they let one person sit in a booth-for-four for two and a half hours over a cup of coffee (pronounced "*caw*-fee").

166

[32–33] – Williamsburg Bridge. From Clinton and Delancey streets across the East River to Brooklyn. Lower East Side, Downtown Manhattan. Leffert Lefferts Buck, engineer. 1930.

Until the coming of Williamsburg Bridge there were only ferries and Brooklyn Bridge linking Manhattan with Brooklyn. The new East River Bridge, or Williamsburg Bridge, as it came to be known, with a 1,600-foot over-water span, was the world's longest suspension bridge in its day and the East River's first all-steel bridge. Its two roadways, two sidewalks, and six tracks for surface and elevated cars formed a highway from the over-crowding of the Lower East Side to the wide-open spaces of Brooklyn. In 1924, the peak year, 505,000 people were crossing daily. *Spanning the 21st Century/Reconstructing A World Class Bridge Program*/A Report to Mayor Edward I. Koch, New York Department of Transportation, 1988, a draft copy of which was obtained by the photographer, identified the problem with regard to the more than 2,000 bridges in New York City: despite recent infusions of reconstruction funds, "currently, New York City bridges receive virtually no preventative maintenance," which, in the case of Williamsburg Bridge, so the DOT concluded, would inevitably result in the bridge having to be replaced at a possible cost of up to $1 billion 1987 dollars.

(*left*) The busy steps at the Delancey Street entrance to the elevated walkway.

(*right*) Pedestrians on the elevated walkway pass by the vast housing projects on the Lower East Side.

[35] – Confucius Plaza, 19 Bowery, Chinatown, Downtown Manhattan.

A behemoth, the huge, curving, red-brick complex named Confucius Plaza, the most modern residential development in Chinatown when it was built in 1976, towers over Division Street.

[36] – Steeple, St Paul's Chapel, between Broadway, Fulton, Church, and Vesey streets, *and* South Tower Building, World Trade Center, between Church, Vesey, West, and Liberty streets, Financial District, Downtown Manhattan.

The closely spaced aluminium facing of the 110-storey World Trade Center Tower, built 1970-77, is a perfect foil for James Crommelin Lawrence's elegant steeple, added to St Paul's Chapel in 1794, pleasingly patterned by scaffolding. One hundred years before, in the summer of 1861, J. H. Beal, with a photographic studio in nearby Beekman Place, came to record repairs to St Paul's Chapel. His photograph, showing the steeple completely enclosed in scaffolding, is reproduced in Mary Black's *Old New York in Early Photographs 1853-1901/196 Prints from the Collection of The New York Historical Society* (1973; second revised edition 1976). Mary Black writes in the Introduction, "One of the questions the Director of The New York Historical Society asked me when I joined the staff in July, 1970 was whether I thought I could organize an exhibition that would introduce the general public to the photographs in the Society's collection. Although neither a New Yorker nor a historian of photography, I had a good idea of the magnitude of such a project." Having accepted the challenge, the Curator of Painting and Sculpture soon found herself sifting more than 50,000 negatives, an even greater number of new and old photographic prints, and "the French photographer Victor Prevost's wax paper negatives, made in

1853 and 1854 and apparently the oldest photographic views of the city," in the Society's photographic archive, formally begun in 1906. As Mary Black also notes, "The resulting exhibition, called *Eye on the City*, was held at the Society from October, 1970 to March, 1971. The present book is an outgrowth of that exhibition, an assembling of its most significant pictures and descriptions in permanent form."

By 1980, when the photographer made an appointment to show a portfolio of his work to Mary Black, it was understood that the Society's Curator of Painting and Sculpture had a keen appreciation of photography. At that first meeting, early in his career as a photographer, it was therefore encouraging to be invited to contribute to a mixed media show at the Society that fall, *The Phrenology of the Land: How to Read the New York Landscape*, 5 September-30 October 1980; and to be promised participation in a major exhibition of contemporary photography of the city which Mary was planning for the following year, *Manhattan Observed: 14 Photographers Look at New York*, 1 July-1 October 1981 (extended to 1 April 1982) and The New York State Museum, Albany, New York, 15 May-15 November 1982. At Mary's invitation, the photographer also contributed to a major photographic exhibition which she guest-curated for the Municipal Art Society, *Images of Brooklyn Bridge: A Centennial Salute by Seven Photographers*, The Urban Center, 457 Madison Avenue, 18 April-24 May (extended to 10 June) 1983.

[37] – An overhead view of Confucius Plaza, from the roof of the Braveman Building, 2 East Broadway, NE corner Catherine Street, Chinatown, Downtown Manhattan.

Confucius. Bronze sculpture; granite pedestal. Liu Shih, sculptor.

A representation of the famous philosopher Confucius (531-479 BC), the proponent of such enduring, Confucian, values as deference to family and to elders, stands in Confucius Plaza at the heart of Chinatown, one of the largest Oriental communities in North America.

[38] – 649-659 Broadway, SoHo, Downtown Manhattan.

Construction workers begin the task of reconstructing a building in the SoHo Historic Cast-Iron District following a devastating fire.

Cast-iron achieved its greatest popularity in the United States between 1880 and 1890, and its use in commercial building, for structural as well as ornamental purposes, reached its heyday in this area of New York. Lighter and cheaper than stone, cast-iron could be mass-produced from standardised moulds and quickly built in any number of architectural styles. Once painted, it was weatherproof and required little maintenance beyond a fresh coat of paint. The elimination of thick walls made large windows and therefore better light and ventilation possible.

The largest remaining group of cast-iron buildings in the world was threatened with destruction by a proposal to construct the Lower Manhattan Expressway which would have driven a 10-lane, straight line through SoHo, Greenwich Village, Little Italy, and the Lower East Side. Driving it forward was New York's autocratic construction tsar Robert Moses, nicknamed by the press "Bob the Big Builder," and, in the words of Jan Morris, "dreaming of huge expressways, tunnels and towers, obliterating neighbourhoods, moving people here and there and making Manhattan the first true auto-city, where the private car had priority over public transport. His attitudes were lordly. Never having learnt to drive a car himself, he maintained a staff of twenty-four-hour chauffeurs, and had offices all over the city, some of them with private dining rooms and chefs ... and he once held twelve city, state and federal jobs all at the same time" (*Manhattan '45*, 1987). The most vocal critic of his entire planning philosophy was Jane Jacobs, a journalist with the now-defunct *Architectural Forum*, Greenwich Village resident, and author of *The Death and Life of Great American Cities* (1961). She showed great skill, as well as commitment to principle, in mobilising community opposition to the ludicrous scheme, which was abandoned, finally, only after a long-drawn-out fight, in 1965.

[39] – Shutters, Jersey Street, between Lafayette and Mulberry streets, SoHo, Downtown Manhattan.

[40–41] – Twin Towers, World Trade Center, Downtown Manhattan

with

(*left*) Woolworth Building, 233 Broadway, between Barclay Street and Park Place. Cass Gilbert (1859-1934), architect. 1913.

Frank W. Woolworth paid $13.5 million in cash for the building, intended as a huge "sky sign" for the chain of five-and-ten cent stores he founded. The 792-foot-high, 60-storey skyscraper, a steel-framed structure, with carved terracotta skin, weathered green copper roof, and spiked crown, was called the "Cathedral of Commerce." Cass Gilbert's Gothic Revival masterpiece, seen here from Williamsburg Bridge, was the tallest building in the world until the Chrysler Building, completed in 1930, took the title.

and

(*right*) A fire escape on Greenwich Street.

[42] – An uncapped fire hydrant, the outflow of water frozen solid in the subzero temperatures of an especially bitter winter. Washington Heights, Uptown Manhattan.

[43] – Water tower, the roof of the Braveman Building, 2 East Broadway, NE corner Catherine Street, Chinatown, *with* Municipal Building, 1 Centre Street, at Chambers Street, *and* Twin Towers, World Trade Centre, between Church, Vesey, West, and Liberty streets, Downtown Manhattan.

As demonstrated by artists Edward Hopper and André Kertesz, the rooftop water tower, a visible part of the skyline since the 1900s, is as emblematic of New York, as at street level, the clouds of white steam that issue from manhole covers and hatches. Architects have gone to great lengths to disguise the essential but utilitarian water tower, a stout cedar tank on spindly legs, with all manner of additions to the city's skyline – cupolas, domes, and spires, among them.

[44–45] – Brooklyn Bridge. From Frankfort Street and Park Row (City Hall Park) east across the East River to Brooklyn.

(*left*) A view from the roof of the Municipal Building of the cat's-cradle of roads that has built up around the approach to the bridge, which, in 1883, had dominated the New York skyline. A print from this period shows the original two outer lanes for horse-drawn carriages, two middle lanes for cable cars, and the elevated centre walkway.

(*right*) The walkway, with its breathtaking views, through the filigree of cables, of the city and the bay, is one of the most worthwhile experiences New York has to offer. Over 15 feet in width, and built 18 feet above the roadway, the pedestrian promenade was thought of by the creator of the bridge, John Roebling, as an important amenity. In his plan of 1867 he wrote that it "would allow people of leisure, and old and young invalids, to promenade over the Bridge on fine days, in order to enjoy the beautiful views and the pure air." He added, "I need not state that in a crowded commercial city, such a promenade will be of incalculable value." Walt Whitman said of it that the view from the walkway was "the most effective medicine my soul has yet partaken." To this day New Yorkers bike, jog, and stroll the unique walkway, reconstructed at the cost of $1 million in 1982.

[46] – Metropolitan Life Insurance Headquarters, east side, 1893; tower, 1909, Napoleon Le Brun & Sons; north building (11-25 Madison Avenue), Midtown Manhattan. Harvey Wiley Corbett and D. Everett Waid, 1932, architects; remodelling, Lloyd Morgan, 1962.

Within less than a decade following completion, in 1902, of the Fuller Building (known as the "Flatiron"), the "skyscraper" was outclassed by its neighbour, fronting the park on Madison Avenue, the Metropolitan Life Insurance Building, whose 700-foot-high, 50-storey tower, New York's great campanile, was the tallest building in the world. The tower clock has four faces – each 26½ feet in diameter – with minute hands weighing a thousand pounds each and hour hands seven hundred pounds. The four enormous chimes, the largest of which weighs seven thousand pounds, sound a measure by Handel every quarter-hour from seven in the morning until ten at night, when a beacon light takes over the watch, flashing red for the quarter hours and white for the hours. The building is connected to a smaller annexe by a covered bridge high above 24th Street.

[47] – George Washington Bridge, from 178th to 179th streets across the Hudson River to Fort Lee, New Jersey, Washington Heights, Uptown Manhattan. Othmar H. Ammann (1879-1965), engineer. Cass Gilbert (1859-1934), architect. 1927-31. Second deck, 1982.

A view west from the Manhattan shore, of the Hudson River, ice carried by its strong currents, part of the bridge's great span, and the tower on the New Jersey side, outlined against the Palisades.

Unlike Brooklyn Bridge, the first steel suspension bridge with its Gothic stone towers, built in a style later called Picturesque Eclectic, George Washington Bridge is all of steel. Like Brooklyn Bridge, George Washington Bridge is not only one of the most remarkable engineering achievements of all time, it is also a spectacular work of pure sculptural art. John Roebling, creator of Brooklyn Bridge, in 1868 said that the Hudson River could be crossed. However, it was not until the 1920s that O. H. Ammann, having previously scouted several possibilities, recognised the 179th Street site as a natural location because of the topography – the Palisades on the New Jersey side, and Washington Heights on the Manhattan side, providing approaches at a height that allowed adequate clearance. In 1927 work was begun. When it opened in 1931, George Washington Bridge was the longest suspension bridge in the world (until completion of the San Francisco-Oakland Bay and Golden Gate bridges). The George Washington has a channel span of 3,500 feet and a total overall length of 4,700 feet, a deck about 115 feet in width and about 250 feet above high water, and towers 600 feet in height. The great, high towers were to have been covered in concrete – Cass Gilbert, the architect, had even designed a Beaux-Arts encasement. However, partly due to pressure from the public and for reasons of cost – the Port Authority of New York and New Jersey had put up the $59 million it cost to build the bridge – the design proposal was rejected at the last minute, thus enabling Le Corbusier, like Ammann, Swiss-born, to rhapsodise, "The George Washington Bridge over the Hudson is the most beautiful bridge in the world. Made of cables and steel beams, it gleams in the sky like a reversed arch. It is blessed. It is the only seat of grace in the disordered city" (*When the Cathedrals Were White*, 1947). And forty years later, Jan Morris, in *Manhattan '45* (1987) penned this piquant postscript:

> "Its designer, the Swiss-born O. H. Ammann (1879-1965), had already built the Triboro and several other New York bridges, and was to go on to build the Verrazano Narrows, the greatest of them all. In his old age, his widow once told me, he liked to sit in his penthouse in the Carlyle Hotel looking at them all through a telescope."

[48] – *Queen Elizabeth I Memorial* (detail), Orient Overseas Building Plaza, 88 Pine Street, Downtown Manhattan. Yu Yu Yang, sculptor. I. M. Pei (1917-), architect of the plaza. 1974. Stainless steel in two unjointed units.

The two-part environmental sculpture commemorates the RMS *Elizabeth*, the largest and fastest ocean liner ever built, which caught fire and sank in Hong Kong Harbour in 1972. One section of the work is a 14,000-pound, L-shaped piece, 21 feet long, 16 feet high, and 2½ feet wide, with a circular opening 12 feet in diameter. The other section, positioned behind the opening, is a vertical disc, weighing 4,000 pounds, 12 feet in diameter, 2½ feet thick, and having a mirror finish. On a pedestal of Italian marble is a plaque with the ship's history.

[49] – (*above*) Chrysler Building, *and* Grand Hyatt Hotel, 42nd Street, between Lexington and Park avenues. Gruzen and Partners, with Der Scutt, architects, 1980 *and* Park Avenue viaduct, completed 1919. Midtown Manhattan.

With its Art Deco spire, the Chrysler is the ultimate symbol of the Jazz Age. The sleek, mirror-like quality of stainless steel made it a favourite building material, even though it was extremely expensive. The beacon cast its elegantly fretted glow on the New York night sky for the first time in the 1980s, thanks to the happy discovery – during the restoration of the building – of the original, but until then, never-implemented, lighting scheme amid the architect's drawings.

The Grand Hyatt, Chrysler's near neighbour, the first of the Trumpian *grands projets* perpetrated in Manhattan, is an H-shaped, 30-storey structure sheathed in silver mirror glass, with a second-floor sidewalk café cantilevered over East 42nd Street; it replaced the old Commodore Hotel.

(*below*) *Ideogram*. James Rosati, sculptor. A shining steel variation on an open rectangle, 1973. Austin J. Tobin Plaza, One and Two World Trade Center (North and South Tower Buildings), Downtown Manhattan.

The vast open space of the five-acre World Trade Center Plaza, designed to provide a park-like setting for office workers and visitors, was enlivened by such specially commissioned pieces of sculpture.

[50–51] – Old St Patrick's Cathedral, between Mott, Prince, and Mulberry streets, Little Italy, Downtown Manhattan. Joseph Mangin, architect, 1815; restoration: Henry Engelbert, 1868.

Originally founded in 1809, the first St Patrick's, built in the Gothic Revival style by Joseph Mangin, co-architect of City Hall, is one of the oldest churches in the city. Catholics and Protestants battled in the streets on Election Day, 12 April 1842, when a No Popery mob attacked the cathedral and stoned the bishop's palace. At issue was a bill in the state legislature allowing public moneys to be diverted to the parochial schools. St Patrick's was substantially rebuilt following a disastrous fire in the 1860s. It continued to flourish after the decision by the Archdiocese of New York in 1879 to relocate the cathedral uptown, to the far grander building designed by James Renwick Jr, on Fifth Avenue. Today, St Patrick's, as the local parish church, serves a continually changing ethnic community.

(*left*) The cemetery.

(*right*) The rebuilt church, from the corner of Mulberry and Spring streets.

[53] – David N. Dinkins, Twenty-fifth Anniversary Graduation, College of Insurance, aboard *The Spirit of New York*, East River, Pier 11, South Street, between Gouverneur and Jones lanes, Downtown Manhattan, 5 June 1987.

David Dinkins, Manhattan Borough President, donned a gold-tasselled academic cap – not seen here – and black silk academic gown to attend this graduation ceremony in 1987. Two years later, in the Democratic primary, he succeeded in ousting the increasingly divisive, right-wing Mayor, Edward I. Koch (catchphrase, "How'm I doin'?"). Having campaigned with the mantra "New York needs a Mayor who will unite the diverse groups who make up the gorgeous mosaic of our city," he went on, in the general election in November 1989, to win the top job, becoming the first African-American Mayor of New York City.

[54] – *The Spirit of Commerce*. Canal Street approach to Manhattan Bridge, Downtown Manhattan. One of two granite groups with ornamental compositions. Carl Augustus Heber, sculptor. Carrère & Hastings, architects. 1916.

Manhattan Bridge, a steel suspension bridge designed by engineer O. F. Nichols, opened in 1909. After Brooklyn and Williamsburg bridges, it was the third suspension bridge to span the East River. The approach is a grand Beaux-Arts stone portal comprising a triumphal arch and curving colonnade, a baroque composition inspired by the Porte Saint-Denis in Paris and the Bernini colonnade that forms the Piazza of St Peter's in Rome. Guarding the approach are two vigorously modelled groups: *Commerce* is portrayed on the north pier as a winged female figure, with, on her right, a kneeling male figure, a hammer in his right hand and a half-covered wheel in his left.

[55] – *Transportation*. Grand Central Terminal, 42nd Street, at Park Avenue, Midtown Manhattan. Statuary group. Bedford Indiana limestone. Jules-Alexis Coutan (1848-1939), sculptor; carving by John Donnelly. Whitney Warren of Warren & Whetmore, architects. 1914.

The elaborate central group, above the clock, crowning Warren's imposing façade – marked by three great arched windows, columns grouped in pairs – has been called "the best piece of monumental sculpture in America" (Henry Hope Reed, *The Golden City*). A 29-foot *Mercury*, backed by an American eagle, personifies Commerce, supported on either side by physical and moral energy, in massive stone figures of *Hercules* and *Minerva*.

Jules-Alexis Coutan, the French sculptor, President, later Dean, of the Académie des Beaux-Arts in Paris, was considered one of the greatest sculptors of his time in the use of the human figure. He was recommended by Warren to William Vanderbilt, who controlled the New York Central Railroad. Donnelly had previously carved the stonework on the Vanderbilt mansions in New York and Rhode Island.

The impact of Warren's magnificent Terminal, a Beaux-Arts building, massive in scale, handsome in proportion, and dignified and restrained in detail, was lessened by the erection over some of Grand Central's air rights in 1963 of the 59-storey, precast concrete Pan Am Building (from 1981, MetLife Building). A plan to demolish Grand Central Terminal and erect a modern commercial structure on the site was the subject of a long legal battle, which ended only when the US Supreme Court upheld the city's right to declare the building a landmark in 1978.

[56–57] – Young mothers with little boys:

(*left*) Hitting the shops, Lower East Side, Downtown Manhattan.

(*right*) Waiting for a bus, Broadway, Upper West Side, Uptown Manhattan.

[58] – A conversation piece, Park Row, Lower East Side, Downtown Manhattan.

> "It is possible in a city-street neighbourhood to know all kinds of people, without unwelcome entanglements, without boredom, necessity for excuses, explanations, fears of giving offence, embarrassments respecting impositions or commitments, and all such paraphernalia of obligations which can accompany less limited relationships."

Jane Jacobs, The Death and Life of Great American Cities, 1961

[59] – A private moment, Mott Street, Chinatown, Downtown Manhattan.

[60] – A view west from Wall Street, at William Street, toward Trinity Church, Broadway, opposite the intersection of Wall Street, Financial District, Downtown Manhattan, 1 April 1980.

On April Fool's Day in Gotham, when 33,000 city bus and subway workers struck, thousands crossed Brooklyn Bridge on foot and hundreds piled onto fishing and tour boats to get to work in Downtown Manhattan. At the foot of the Wall Street canyon, a New York City Transit Police Department officer secures the – closed – entrance to the subway on Wall Street, NE corner William Street.

Henry James characterised New York City in *The American Scene*, the record of his visit in 1904-05 after twenty-five years of expatriation, as a place of "pitiless ferocity"; and nowhere with more arrogance than in the skyscrapers of Wall Street, those "giants of the marketplace," which had "crushed" the familiar monuments of his youth.

At the head of Wall Street, hemmed in by the high-rise counting houses of what Washington Irving called "the Almighty Dollar," in an incongruous partnering of God and Mammon, stands the Gothic Revival Trinity Church, designed by the English architect Richard Upjohn (1802-78). Trinity Church, New York's most famous church, the third church to have stood on the site, in one of America's oldest parishes, founded in 1697, was built in New Jersey dark red sandstone, commonly called "brownstone," in 1854, with a massive square tower and a 284-foot octagonal steeple that, for fifty years, was the tallest structure in New York. In the little graveyard lie buried some of the distinguished personages who were Trinity's early parishioners, most notable among them the first US Secretary of the Treasury (appointed 1789) Alexander Hamilton, one of the greatest of Americans. "Why has government been instituted at all? Because the passions of men will not conform to the dictates of reason and justice, without constraint," wrote Hamilton in *The Federalist* (1787-88), no. 15.

In New York in the 1980s, the so-called "Greed Decade," in which there was greater wealth inequality and an ever more divided society, Wall Street, the most famous third of a mile in the world, gained notoriety for hostile, insanely leveraged corporate takeovers. The late Tom Wolfe, the leading practitioner of "The New Journalism," in the eerily prescient novel *The Bonfire of the Vanities* (1987), has as his central character a rich bond-salesman, worried that he may not make more than $1 million per, who travels daily to his office so that he, a "Master of the Universe," can maintain isolation from poor people. On quitting the city in favour of Washington DC, Irving Kristol, right-wing commentator with the *Wall Street Journal* and fellow of the American Enterprise Institute, said that, in New York, to be classified as a mere millionaire you need $20 million; to be "rich" you need at least twice that amount; and to be wealthy you need $100 million. In 1986 Wall Street was rocked by scandal, which wreaked havoc on the market, when there were federal prosecutions, as the understaffed and under-financed Securities and Exchange Commission, at long last, aggressively attacked insider trading. Fined a record $100 million was Ivan Boesky, king of the arbitrageurs, who was quoted as saying, "Greed is all right, by the way. I want you to know that. I think greed is healthy. You can be greedy and still feel good about yourself."

> "I know of no country, indeed, where the love of money has taken stronger hold on the affections of men and where a profounder contempt is expressed for the theory of the permanent equality of property."
>
> Alexis de Tocqueville, *Democracy in America*, pt I (1835), ch. 3, The Henry Reeve text, as revised by Francis Bowen, corrected and edited by Phillips Bradley (1945)

[61] – A man in a corner phone booth, Midtown Manhattan.

> "New Yorkers are prodigious talkers; in a city of 7,073,500 residents an average of 43 million calls are dialled each day."
>
> Richard E. Shepard, "Metropolitan Math," "The World of New York," *New York Times Magazine*, Part 2, 28 April 1985

[62] – Boys on a stoop, Little Italy, Downtown Manhattan.

A hand-me-down from the Dutch citizens of New Amsterdam, who spoke of "*stoeps*," the word "stoop," meaning a short flight of steps leading to a platform and the front door of a private home or tenement house, has come to mean New York.

[63] – Young mothers with children in strollers, at a hot dog cart, Sixth Avenue, Midtown Manhattan.

[64–65] – The Garment District, an area between Broadway and Ninth Avenue, south of 40th Street, centred on Seventh Avenue around 34th Street, known as Fashion Avenue, Midtown Manhattan.

Workshops, warehouses, factories, and showrooms line the streets jammed with trucks in a neighbourhood that is crucial to the city's identity. The hub of New York's vital, multi-million-dollar fashion industry, where the hard graft of manufacturing and finishing clothing, especially for women and children, carries on, is, more than anywhere else, perhaps, the place to experience what Jan Morris described in *Manhattan '45* (1987) as "the city's irresistible momentum."

(*left*) A porter with a handtruck is stuck in traffic.

(*right*) A porter pulls a rack to be reloaded at a studio.

[66] – Madonna and child, Rutgers Street, at East Broadway, Lower East Side, Downtown Manhattan.

[67] – A little boy with an umbrella, Ninth Avenue, Chelsea, Midtown Manhattan.

"New Yorkers buy umbrellas whenever it rains, and when the sky clears discard them like outmoded identities, inconvenient memories."

Peter Conrad, *Where I Fell to Earth: A Life in Four Places*, 1990

[68] – Bayard Building, 65 Bleecker Street, between Broadway and Lafayette streets, Downtown Manhattan. Louis Henri Sullivan (1856-1924), architect. 1898.

The architect whom Frank Lloyd Wright called "the master," whose buildings in Chicago and the Middle West counted among the leading structures in the development of modern architecture in America and abroad, is represented in New York by the Bayard Building. The city's sole example of the work of Louis H. Sullivan is a tall building squeezed into a commercial block, which can be truly appreciated only by crossing Bleecker and looking back from a little way down Crosby Street. In what has been described as "an ode to Chicago's love for structural expression," the solid, structural columns that divide the windows culminate, unexpectedly, in a sextet of open-winged angels at the cornice, this last detail added, it is said, over the objection of the architect, who gave in to the wisdom of the building's owner, Silas Alden Condict, for whom it was once named. Given Sullivan's dictum, "Form ever follows function" ("The Tall Building Artistically Considered," *Lippincott's Magazine*, March 1896), it is remarkable how much ornamentation there is, in terracotta, the architect's favourite building material, in evidence here, in the flamboyant, filigreed decoration of the entrance.

[69] – *Bust of Sylvette*. University Village, Greenwich Village, Downtown Manhattan. Concrete, with black basalt pebbles, 36 feet high, 20 feet long, 12½ inches thick, weighing 60 tons. Pablo Picasso (1881-1972), sculptor; Carl

Nesjar, adapting sculptor. Gift of Mr and Mrs Alan D. Emil, 1968. 100–110 Bleecker Street; 505 LaGuardia Place. I. M. Pei & Partners, with James L. Freed in charge, architects. 1966.

New York's only public Picasso sculpture is an adaptation of a 1934 Cubist study of a girl with a ponytail, originally rendered on a 2-foot painted cut-out of bent sheet metal. Nesjar used a reinforced concrete skin, which he etched by sandblasting, revealing the black basalt aggregate beneath the buff surface. The work, set in a square, is the centrepiece of three high-rise apartment buildings by I. M. Pei (1917-), the Chinese-American master of modern architecture. It was Pei who wanted a Picasso sculpture for the space, and it was Picasso who selected *Sylvette* to go there.

[70] – *Group of Four Trees*. Chase Manhattan Plaza, between Nassau, William, Liberty, and Pine streets, Financial District, Downtown Manhattan. Steel framework, covered with a skin of fibreglass and plastic resin, 40 feet high, painted with polyurethane in a linear pattern. Jean Dubuffet (1901-85), sculptor. 1972. Skidmore, Owings & Merrill (Gordon Bunshaft, partner in charge), architects. 1961.

The Chase Manhattan Bank was born of the merger between the Chase National Bank and the Bank of the Manhattan Company. David Rockefeller, president of Chase Manhattan Bank and chairman of the Downtown-Lower Manhattan Association, resolved to save Wall Street with one mighty building. One Chase Manhattan Plaza, the first major new building in the Financial District since 1932, and the first notable example of the International Style to be built Downtown, at 813 feet, was at the time the sixth tallest building in the world, a stately, 60-storey, glass-and-aluminium structure, occupying less than 30 percent of its 2½-acre site, creating an 89,466-square-foot plaza around it. The Revised Zoning Law of 1961 brought plazas and public spaces to the city, resulting in an upsurge of sculpture placed on plazas. Sometimes the sculpture appears to have been an afterthought, a late addition to the building, with no relationship between the two. Jean Dubuffet's *Four Trees*, an immense black-and-white sculpture, light in feeling, only added in 1972 to Chase Manhattan Plaza, in 1961 lower Manhattan's first plaza, plays well against the tall tower of Chase bank. The artist's first outdoor sculpture to be erected in the United States, having been assembled from prefabricated sections made in Dubuffet's studio in Périgny, near Paris, *Trees* is one of the most attractive of modern sculptures in a New York public space.

[71] – A wall-end mural above a concrete playground, East Broadway, Lower East Side, Downtown Manhattan.

A form of urban folk art, probably created in the 1970s, this heroic mural conveys its "power to the people" message, while young men from the famously diverse local community, New York's traditional "Melting Pot," shoot a few hoops. All over the city, real New York-style basketball is concrete playground basketball.

[72–73] – Overviews of 42nd Street, between Lexington and Vanderbilt avenues, from the elevated "circumferential plaza" around Grand Central Terminal.

(*left*) A rainy day on one of the few east-west thoroughfares in the city.

(*right*) Long before the building frenzy of the 1980s, New York was understood to be a developer's paradise. Walt Whitman (1819-92) remarked on the "pull-down-and-build-all-over-again spirit" that prevailed in what he described elsewhere as the "mettlesome, mad, extravagant city." The short-story writer O. Henry (1862-1920), who, famously, described New York as "Baghdad on the Subway," is reputed to have said, "It'll be a great place if they ever finish it." Here, passersby take advantage of "windows" in a perimeter fence to inspect work on the site of the future Kalikow Building, 101 Park Avenue.

> "There's a more or less general notion that sidewalk superintendents – idling citizens who love to study building excavations – were officially recognized for the first time in the Thirties, when Rockefeller Center was building. The recognition is much older than that. John J. Downey, contractor, put up a bulletin in 1858 when he finished foundation construction at 52-56 Broadway, thanking spectators for their kind interest in the building's progress. 'I regret,' his notice concluded, 'that I can no longer entertain you, and must bid you good day.' "
>
> Meyer ("Mike") Berger, *Meyer Berger's New York*, Foreword by Brooks Atkinson, 1960

[74–75] – Youth and Age, Greenwich Village, Downtown Manhattan.

(*left*) Seniors schmooze in a minipark on Sixth Avenue.

(*right*) A young man with mental health issues panhandles at the entrance to Village Cigars, 110 Seventh Avenue, SE corner Christopher Street.

> "Last fall, after almost a decade of dilatory and halfhearted measures to help the homeless, Mayor Koch finally initiated a plan: declare large numbers of the unfortunate street people mentally ill and then sweep them into hospitals. There are state laws that allow the involuntary hospitalization of those deemed to be a danger to themselves or others, and clearly there are a lot of disturbed New Yorkers on the loose among us (many of them, of course, are living on the streets precisely because they have been discharged from hospitals)."
>
> Jamie Malanowski, "Koch's Plan for the Homeless/One Case History," *Spy*, February 1988

[76–77] – Empire State Building, 350 Fifth Avenue, SW corner 34th Street, Midtown Manhattan, *and*

(*left*) framed by the vast projects of the Lower East Side, in a view from Williamsburg Bridge: New York Life Insurance Company Building, 51 Madison Avenue, 26th to 27th streets, Cass Gilbert (1859-1934), architect. 1928.

The Gothic Revival building, with a 617-foot-high tower, topped by a gilt pyramidal roof, occupies the site once occupied by, from the 1830s to the early 1870s, the New York and Harlem (Railroad) Union Depot, and, from 1890, the original Madison Square Garden, the flamboyant palace designed by Stanford White of McKim, Mead & White, that was the largest building in America devoted entirely to amusements. In 1906, while watching a review in the roof garden, White was shot dead by millionaire Harry K. Thaw, the husband of White's former mistress, showgirl Evelyn Nesbit.

(*right*) Marble Collegiate Reformed Church, Fifth Avenue, at 29th Street. Samuel A. Warner, architect. 1854.

From Art Deco to Gothic Revival, a young woman cycles past the two landmark buildings, in markedly different styles of architecture, on Fifth Avenue, with, on the sidewalk, *right*, the Big Apple emblem of New York, a town so big they had to name it twice.

As its name suggests, the church is constructed of marble; "Collegiate," because in its denomination, the oldest in Manhattan, ministers are known as "colleagues." The Collegiate Reformed Dutch Church of the City of New York was founded in 1628 by Dominie Michaëlius, the first pastor in Nieuw Amsterdam, the name given to the settlement established in 1625 as a fur trading post by the Dutch West India Company, whose employee the minister was. Peter Minuit, the second Director-General, or Governor, was Church Elder. In the summer of 1627, Minuit had made his celebrated arrangement with the Algonquian-speaking first inhabitants of "Manahata" or "Manahatin" whereby the Island of Manhattan was purchased by the Dutch West India Company for trading goods worth sixty guilders – the famous $24 as calculated by nineteenth-century historians. The fortieth minister in succession to pastor Dominie Michaëlius, Dr Norman Vincent Peale, gave a phrase to the language as the author of the phenomenally best-selling *Power of Positive Thinking*.

[78–79] – Flatiron Building, 175 Fifth Avenue, at Broadway and 23rd Street. D. H. Burnham & Co., architects. 1902.

While Chicago gave birth to the skyscraper, New York has seen some of its greatest innovations. One such was the Flatiron Building, one of New York's most famous early skyscrapers – and, when completed in 1902, the tallest building in the world – built by Daniel Hudson Burnham (1846-1912), one of Chicago's great modernists. On the acute-angled triangle made by the scissor-like intersection of Broadway and Fifth Avenue at 23rd Street rose the 21-storey Flatiron Building, one of the first buildings to use a steel frame, clad in rusticated limestone, and, at 286 feet, so tall that sceptics said it would collapse. The triangle-shaped structure, originally named the Fuller Building for its owner George Fuller, was dubbed the Flatiron Building because of its resemblance to the domestic object, and the building adopted its nickname as its official title.

(*left*) A view west toward the Hudson River from the roof of the Metropolitan Life Building, 1 Madison Avenue, reveals the elaborate detailing of the rusticated limestone façade, reminiscent of an Italian Renaissance palazzo.

(*right*) A head-on view, at street level from the west side of Madison Square, highlights the unique form of the building, triangular in plan, only 6 feet wide at the apex.

[80–81] – Walking to the corner (a New York "thing").

> "…the most elemental of New York's attractions – the life of its streets. Visitors of every era have remarked on this but never has the street life been more vigorous. The pace is set by New York's pedestrians and it is fast, now averaging about three hundred feet per minute. They are skilful, too, using hand and eye signals, feints and sidesteps to clear the track ahead. They are natural jaywalkers, sneaking across on the diagonal while tourists wait docilely on the corner for the light. It is the tourists, moreover, who are vexing, with their ambiguous moves and their maddeningly slow gait. They put New Yorkers off their game."

> William H. Whyte, A New Introduction, *The WPA Guide to New York City/ The Federal Writers Project Guide to 1930s New York*, 1939, reissued 1982

(*left, above*) One man and his dog (er, canine companion), an intersection, Midtown Manhattan.

Eighties New York experienced Big Dog syndrome, the replacement of "handbag" breeds by bigger and bigger breeds, often dangerous and always expensive, perceived by non-canophiles as an invasion of city culture by the suburbs.

(*left, below*) A dance to the music of time, Eighth Avenue, SW corner 33rd Street, Midtown Manhattan, the precast-concrete-clad drum of Madison Square Garden Center in shadow, while over on Fifth Avenue, the Empire State Building, the Eighth Wonder of the World, radiates light. "Street ballet" in New York is synchronicity, not choreography.

(*right, above*) The New Yorker does not break stride. Lower East Side, Downtown Manhattan.

(*right, below*) A woman passes "WALL OF RESPECT FOR WOMEN," a mural, Rutgers Street, at East Broadway, Lower East Side.

The photographer began life in New York as a bohemian expatriate, near here, in a fourth-floor walkup at 162 East Broadway, above the last subway stop in Manhattan of the F train to Brooklyn, catty-corner from the 11-storey tower of the *Jewish Daily Forward* (*Forverts* in Yiddish), which, since 1897, had been at once the mouthpiece and the guardian of immigrants.

> "No one should come to New York to live unless he is willing to be lucky."

> E. B. White

[82] – A meeting by the bins. An apartment building, Downtown Manhattan.

[83] – Catherine Street, with a tugboat on the East River passing below Brooklyn Bridge, from the roof of the Braveman Building, 2 East Broadway, NE corner Catherine Street, Chinatown, Downtown Manhattan.

[85] – A romantic interlude, near the Morgan Library, East 36th Street, between Park and Madison avenues, Murray Hill, Midtown Manhattan.

[86–87] – Brooklyn Botanic Garden, 1000 Washington Avenue, Middle Brooklyn. Opposite the eastern edge of Prospect Park, Brooklyn Botanic Garden – with 12,000 different kinds of plants growing in its 50 acres – is devoted to the collection, study, and interpretation of plants for the education and enjoyment of all.

(*left*) Administration Building (former Laboratory Building), Conservatory Plaza. McKim, Mead & White, architects. 1918. At the heart of one of New York's best-loved cultural institutions is the elegant, two-storey, white stone and stucco Administration Building, each of its central and wing sections surmounted by an octagonal cupola. In Conservatory Plaza, a formal garden of magnolias and stone vases, are two rectangular lily-pools, one containing tropical varieties, the other, hardy specimens.

(*right*) Two well-dressed visitors to the Botanic Garden, seated on a carved stone bench.

[88] – *The Army, Soldiers' and Sailors' Memorial Arch*. Grand Army Plaza, Middle Brooklyn. Frederick William MacMonnies (1863-1937), sculptor (three bronze groups); Thomas Eakins and William Rudolph O'Donovan, sculptors (bronze reliefs). John Hemingway Duncan, architect. The cornerstone was laid by General William Tecumseh Sherman in 1889, and the arch was completed in 1892. Granite arch, 80 feet in height and width, enclosing an archway 50 feet high, and with a span of 35 feet and a depth of 50 feet along the base.

Inscription:

TO THE DEFENDERS OF THE UNION, 1861-1865

The arch, one of the great memorial arches of the modern era, is crowned at the top of the arch by MacMonnies' *Victory*, comprising a triumphant female figure borne in a quadriga and flanked by winged trumpeters. Two other colossal groups, *The Army* and *The Navy*, rest in front of the piers on pedestals, ornamented with columns. In the first of these, seen here, the sculptor has created an agitated contour of lights, shadows, and bristling bayonets – he said that he conceived the group as an "explosion." In the background, the winged female figure represents Bellona, the goddess of war. The forward figure, with raised sword, is a self-portrait of MacMonnies. The group was inspired by Delacroix's landmark painting *Liberty Guiding the People*.

Brooklyn-born MacMonnies' boyhood interest in modelling small figures and animals led to an apprenticeship in the studio of Dublin-born Augustus Saint-Gaudens. Promoted to the position of an assistant, he also attended the National Academy of Design and the Art Students League, and eventually went to Paris and studied under Alexandre Falguière at the École des Beaux-Arts. As one of the three leading American sculptors, along with Saint-Gaudens and Daniel Chester French, he took an active role in the Columbian Exposition at Chicago in 1893.

[89] – *The Horse Tamers*. Park Circle entrance, Prospect Park, Middle Brooklyn. One of two bronze groups on ornamented granite pedestals. Frederick William MacMonnies (1863-1937), sculptor. Stanford White (1853-1906), architect. 1899.

Characteristic of Beaux-Arts sculpture, MacMonnies' *Horse Tamers* reflects the prevailing interest in representing abstract ideas through naturalistic images. In this case, the muscular, youthful riders on each of the groups, straining to keep the rearing horses in check, represent the mind of man pitted against brute force. When plaster casts of them were exhibited at the Paris Exposition in 1900 and the Pan-American Exposition in 1901 the two groups attracted great attention. Today, these large, neo-baroque groups, on pedestals designed by Stanford White, the architect who procured for MacMonnies this commission, as he had for the colossal groups on the *Soldiers' and Sailors' Memorial Arch*, can be appreciated for the sheer bravura of the sculptor's performance.

[90–91] – The Abby Aldrich Rockefeller Sculpture Garden, The Museum of Modern Art, 11 West 53rd Street, Midtown Manhattan. Philip L. Goodwin and Edward Durrell Stone, architects. 1939; additions: Philip Johnson (1906-2005), 1951, 1964. Reopened after a $58 million renovation doubled the gallery space, 17 May 1984.

Founded by wealthy patrons in 1919, the world-renowned Museum of Modern Art is one of New York's great International Style structures. The sculpture garden at MoMA – the original layout by Philip Johnson has undergone changes to the design of Cesar Pelli – a graceful mix of fountains, platforms, pools, and plantings, all in perfect balance with one another and the works of art displayed therein, is one of the best open spaces in the city.

(*left*) *The River*. Aristide Maillol (1861-1944), sculptor.

(*right*) *Monument to Balzac*. Auguste Rodin (1840-1917), sculptor.

[92–93] – Brooklyn Bridge (details), from South Street, between the elevated FDR Drive and the East River, Downtown Manhattan.

Beginning in the early part of the nineteenth century, the great age of sail, and lasting for more than fifty years, a period of intense growth and activity was brought about very largely by the opening of the Erie Canal in 1825: New York, the gateway to the Great Lakes and the West, became a leading port. A popular saying was "All roads lead to South Street," and South Street, lined with the tall masts of sailing ships from all over the world, was known as "the street of ships." Then, with the advent of steam-driven ships in the 1860s, the commercial area shifted to the North River, as the Hudson River was then called. Over time, the shore of the East River had been pushed back relentlessly. Pearl Street was the original shoreline; everything between Pearl and the River is landfill. Since the 1930s, when Manhattan became the first auto-city, and the island's precious littoral was handed over for highways, South Street has been overpowered by the oppressive elevated FDR Drive.

(*left*) The great sweep of the bridge's central span, the catenary curve of the steel cables, and the vast, granite, Gothic Brooklyn tower form the dramatic backdrop to the scene of children at play beside the river at high tide.

(*right*) The elevated FDR carves a curving path past the bridge toward the towers of the Financial District, leaving behind the seated figure of an old seafarer contemplating beside the river at low tide.

[94] – *José Julian Martí* (detail). Central Park South and Sixth Avenue. Bronze equestrian sculpture; granite pedestal. Anna Vaughn Hyatt Huntington (1876-1973), sculptor. 1965.

Inscription:

Apostle of Cuban Independence, leader of the peoples of America and defender of human dignity. His literary genius vied with his political foresight. He was born in Havana on January 28, 1853. For fifteen years of his exile he lived in the City of New York. He died in action at Dos Ríos in Oriente Province on May 19, 1895.

Hyatt's love for, and study of, animals was encouraged by her zoologist father. She received art instruction at the Art Students League, at Syracuse University, and with (John) Gutzon Borglum, famous for his portrait heads of the four Presidents on Mount Rushmore, who had taken up sculpture to explore his interest in depicting wild animals. An accomplished horsewoman, Hyatt had a thorough knowledge of animal movements and anatomy, as is evident in a number of equestrian portraits, among them *Joan of Arc* (1915), Riverside Drive and 93rd Street, and *The Cid Campeador* (1927), The Hispanic Society of America, Audubon Terrace, Broadway, 155th to 156th streets. Her statue of Rodrigo de Vivar, the eleventh-century hero who fought against the Moors in Spain, is one of a number of works by Hyatt, in bronze, marble, and limestone, in the court of The Hispanic Society of America. The cultural centre on Washington Heights, of which The Hispanic Society of America, founded in 1904, forms part, came into being through the liberality of Hyatt's husband, the poet, scholar, and philanthropist Arthur Milton Huntington, who inherited the fortune amassed by his father, Collis P. Huntington, railroad magnate and developer of the Newport News Shipbuilding Company. At the suggestion of her husband, Hyatt portrayed the Cuban writer and revolutionary hero José Martí at the exact moment he was shot and mortally wounded.

[95] – *William Tecumseh Sherman* (detail). Grand Army Plaza, Fifth Avenue, at 59th Street, Midtown Manhattan. Bronze group; polished pink granite pedestal with three bronze wreaths. Augustus Saint-Gaudens (1848-1907), sculptor. Charles Follen McKim, architect. Unveiled 30 May 1903.

One of the most successful generals of the Civil War, William Tecumseh Sherman (1820-91) is represented by

Saint-Gaudens as a caped figure on horseback, led, on foot, by the symbolic, winged, female figure of Victory. Mathew Brady photographed Sherman in 1865, the year of final Union victory, following his "march to the sea" of 1864 that made him a hero to the North but anathema to the South. In command of 100,000 men, Sherman had captured Atlanta by 2 September 1864, and, on 17 October, set off from that devastated city for Savannah, the imperturbable general marching 62,000 men without supplies on a march that was one of deliberate and disciplined destruction. "Where our footsteps pass," wrote one of his aides, "fire, ashes, and desolation follow."

In 1892, a year after the general's death, the eminent Dublin-born sculptor Saint-Gaudens, a product of the École des Beaux-Arts in Paris, received a commission from the Sherman Monument Committee to model the statue of Sherman. Preoccupied with other commissions at the time, the sculptor was not able to give his full attention to the *Sherman*. In 1897 he returned to Paris to begin work on the project in his studio there. He based his portrait of Sherman on a bust of the general he had executed in New York in 1888. Is it possible that Saint-Gaudens also saw the Brady photograph of his subject which, as was said of the photographer's study of a troubled President Lincoln in May 1861, "began to reveal his inner torment as lines of travail etched his features"? The cost of the war, in human terms, had been colossal. Deaths from all causes in the two armies totalled some 620,000, and thousands more were wounded.

The classic winged figure of Victory, represented by Saint-Gaudens leading the general forward, went through several versions: the head and wind-blown draperies were problematic, as was the forward movement. A full-size plaster model of the monument was completed in time for the Paris Exposition in 1900, where it was awarded a Grand Prix. A perfectionist, Saint-Gaudens continued to rework the sculpture at his studio in New Hampshire, sending his improvement to the Paris foundry to be incorporated into the group. With the final alterations made, the piece was cast and then shipped to New England, where a double coat of gold leaf was applied. The gilt bronze group was sent to New York, where, after initial difficulties about its site had been resolved, it was located in the northern part of Grand Army Plaza, the section of Fifth Avenue in front of the Plaza Hotel, New York's first urban plaza, and at the southern entrance to Central Park, known as Scholar's Gate. The group, photographed before restoration and re-gilding, was the climax of Saint-Gaudens's long and distinguished career. It is considered to be one of the great equestrian monuments in Western art.

[96–97] – The waterfront, at the foot of Christopher Street and Morton Street pier, Far West Village, Downtown Manhattan.

Several oyster barges were once more or less permanent adornments along the Hudson at the foot of Christopher Street, just north of the Hoboken Ferry slip and the White Star pier. The elevated West Side Highway, closed to traffic, 15 December 1973, and subsequently demolished, defined the area in which New Yorkers came up for air.

(*left, above*) A manspreading young man sports a self-identifying belt-buckle.

(*left, below*) Spectators of the paseo, Easter Sunday, 1980.

(*right, above and below*) New Yorkers chill out, Easter Sunday, 1980.

[98–99] – The waterfront, at the foot of Christopher Street, Far West Village, Downtown Manhattan.

(*left*) Carl, Easter Sunday, 1980.

(*right, above*) Two young women step out.

(*right, below*) "Roller-Arena," Easter Sunday, 1980.

> "Toto, I've a feeling we're not in Kansas anymore."

Noel Langley, *The Wizard of Oz* (screenplay), 1939,
spoken by Judy Garland as Dorothy Gale

[100] – The area of the old meat-packing district, an agglomeration of tumbledown loft buildings, and rows of decrepit metal canopies, the farther reaches of the Far West Village, Downtown Manhattan.

(*above*) HIDE-A-WAY MOTEL, West 14th Street, between 10th Avenue and Eleventh Avenue (as the waterfront street is known). A dubious-looking establishment occupies a triangular site in the boondocks.

(*below*) "Sleaze" – the USP of a hardcore night club is signalled by this poster-covered wall.

[101] – A gay man cruises a derelict Hudson River pier building torched by arsonists.

> "In the dim, labyrinthine ruin, people enacted their dreams."

Peter Conrad, *Where I Fell to Earth: A Life in Four Places*, 1990

[103] – The Ramble, Central Park. Frederick Law Olmsted (1822-1903) and Calvert Vaux (1824-95), co-designers. 1857-73.

A steep, well-wooded, rugged hillside, intersected by winding paths, and bordered by the Lake, the 37-acre Ramble, of all areas of the 843-acre, man-made Central Park, 2½ miles long and ½ mile wide, comes closest to fulfilling the aim of its creator, Olmsted, a pioneer in the new profession of "landscape architecture," to take the city dweller out of his or her urban surroundings and experience the joy in nature. It has been observed that "Olmsted was a complex character: a man with the imagination and sensitivity of an artist and the iron will of an executive; an idealist, a perfectionist with a driving social conscience ... [whose] approach to landscape was not purely aesthetic. Everything he set his hand to was directly concerned with human welfare" (Paul

Brooks, "Yosemite: The Seeing Eye and the Written Word," Introduction, *Anselm Adams and the Range of Light*, A Special Introduction prepared by New York Graphic Society for the Museum of Modern Art, New York, 1979). The "Greensward Plan," the pseudonym adopted by Olmsted and Vaux for their submission to the Board of Commissioners of the Central Park, which was awarded the $2,000 prize, 28 April 1858, was accompanied by a Report in which the author stated: "It is of great importance as the first real park made in this country – a democratic development of the highest significance and on the success of which, in my opinion, much of the progress of art and aesthetic culture in this country is dependent."

The designers of Central Park, central not to the population, most of whom lived south of Forty-second Street, but to the island itself, wanted to create a lush "natural" landscape, in which there was a balance between more "natural" areas for appreciating nature, such as the Ramble, and more formal areas for promenading, such as the neighbouring Bethesda Terrace. To create this vision of *rus in urbe*, a meticulous construction that was guided by their prize-winning "Greensward Plan," a labour force of 3,000 mostly unemployed Irish workers, and 400 horses, had to shift nearly 5 million yards of stone, earth, and topsoil; lay 272 cubic yards of masonry, quarrying half the stone from within the park itself; build 30 bridges and 11 overpasses across the sunken transverse roads; lay 62 miles of drainage pipe and more than 13 miles of water pipe; construct 6.5 miles of carriage drives, 58 miles of paths, and 6 miles of perimeter wall; and plant more than 500,000 trees, shrubs, and vines. Over a 16-year period, at a cost of $14 million (roughly $118 million today), on an unpromising site, Olmsted and Vaux imposed America's first major urban park. Central Park is the only municipal park that is a national historic landmark, and it is the city's first designated scenic landmark.

[104] – A couple at a corner table in the café, Loeb Boathouse, Central Park, Uptown Manhattan.

[105] – A couple beside the lake, the Japanese Hill-and-Pond Garden, Brooklyn Botanic Garden, Middle Brooklyn.

In the lake, shaped like the Chinese letter meaning "heart" (the centre of meditative calm) is a torii, or bird-perching gate, which marks the approach to a Shinto shrine on the rise beyond the Niwa, or landscape garden, designed by Takeo Shiota in 1914. Created in an acre around the lake, it embodies aspects of four kinds of gardens steeped in religious or social tradition – palace, tea cult, Shinto, and Buddhist temple – and is typical of the Japanese talent for condensation.

[106–107] – *The Bailey Fountain* (details). Grand Army Plaza, Middle Brooklyn. Bronze group on rock base in oval fountain. Eugene Francis Savage (1883-1978), sculptor. Egerton Swartout (1870-1943), designer of the base. 1932.

A sculptured group of male and female figures representing *Wisdom* and *Felicity* stands on the prow of a ship surrounded by Neptune and his attendant Tritons and a boy grasping a cornucopia. The fountain was the $125,000 gift of Frank Bailey, local financier and philanthropist.

[108] – A young cyclist, Bethesda Terrace, with a couple in a rowing boat on the Lake, Central Park, Uptown Manhattan.

[109] – *National Maine Monument* (detail), Columbus Circle, intersection of Broadway and Eighth Avenue, Midtown Manhattan. Granite and marble stele, 43½ feet high, supporting bronze and marble sculpture. Attilio Piccirilli (1866-1945), sculptor. H. Van Buren Magonigle, architect. 1913.

On the night of 15 February 1898 the *Maine*, a battleship constructed in Brooklyn Navy Yard in 1890, blew up and sank in Havana Harbour with the loss of 260 American lives, impressing on a horrified nation the catchphrase "Remember the *Maine*!" Spain, whose colonial empire included Cuba, was held responsible, and the event sparked the Spanish-American War. The names of those who perished in the disaster are inscribed on the east and west sides of the pylon. At the top is a 15-foot group, cast from cannon brought up from the sunken battleship, in which a female figure, standing in a shell drawn by three hippocampi, represents *Columbia Triumphant*. At the base, among other symbolic figures created for the monument, on the west side, the reclining figure of an old man with a long, flowing beard represents the Pacific, while on the east, a Michelangelesque reclining youth represents the Atlantic.

> "From the presidency of James K. Polk to that of John Fitzgerald Kennedy, 'the Pearl of the Antilles,' only ninety miles off the Florida coast, tempted and vexed American administrations."
>
> Samuel Eliot Morison, Henry Steele Commager, William E. Leuchtenburg,
> *A Concise History of the American Republic*, An Abbreviated and Newly Revised
> Edition of *The Growth of the American Republic*, 1977

[110–111] – Bethesda Terrace and Fountain. Central Park, Uptown Manhattan. Frederick Law Olmsted (1822-1903) and Calvert Vaux (1824-95), co-designers. 1857-73.

The northern end of the Mall terminates in a balustrade. A sculptured double staircase, terrace, and the central fountain, all designed by Jacob Wrey Mould, are the architectural heart of the park, a formal element in the "natural" landscape.

(*left*) A view south from the Ramble toward Central Park South.

The silhouettes of tall buildings in a misty light bring drama to the landscape. In the 1850s, when the vision of Central Park was being advocated by the journalist and poet William Cullen Bryant, among other prominent New Yorkers, the city ended at Forty-second Street, and well beyond it lay "waste land, ugly and repulsive." Views of the city from the park were something the designers struggled to prevent, and when the city consisted of five- and six-storey houses, they succeeded.

In a city that is a people-watcher's paradise, Bethesda Terrace is pure heaven.

(*right*) *Angel of the Waters* (Bethesda Fountain). Bronze sculpture; granite fountain. Emma Stebbins (1815-82), sculptor. Jacob Wrey Mould (1825-86), designer. 1873.

Against the romantic background of the Lake and the Ramble, Bethesda Fountain plays, presided over by an angel, wings outspread, supported, at the base, by four cherubs – Purity, Health, Temperance, and Peace. The name refers to the biblical account of a healing angel at the pool of Bethesda in Jerusalem. The sculpture marked the opening in 1842 of the Croton Aqueduct system, which brought the city its first supply of pure water. Emma Stebbins, the sculptor, the sister of Henry G. Stebbins, on the Board of Commissioners of Central Park, began her career as a painter in the 1830s and took up sculpture in 1857. After moving to Rome, she joined a group of women sculptors, referred to by Henry James as "the white marmorean flock." The model of the sculpture for Bethesda Fountain was made in the sculptor's studio in Rome and the piece was cast in Munich.

[112–113] – The Lake, Central Park, Uptown Manhattan. Frederick Law Olmsted (1822-1903) and Calvert Vaux (1824-95), co-designers. 1857-73.

(*left*) A view northeast from the wooded shore of the Lake toward Loeb Boathouse and Fifth Avenue, with Carlyle Hotel, 35 East 76th Street, NE corner Madison Avenue. Bien & Prince, architects. 1923.

Not until the twentieth century did the long stretch of Fifth Avenue facing the park achieve its fame as "Millionaires Row." On the affluent Upper East Side, known as "the Golden Ghetto," one of the few skyscrapers of real visual interest is the 38-storey tower, with a conical-topped crown, of the Carlyle, *right*, considered to be New York's best hotel.

(*right*) A view west from the shore of the Lake near Loeb Boathouse toward San Remo, 145-146 Central Park West, between 74th and 75th streets. Emery Roth, architect. 1930.

Built in the golden age of apartment building on Central Park West, New York's grand boulevard, the twin-towered, Art Deco San Remo is one of several palazzo-style houses on the avenue that are home in New York to some of America's top talents in the world of opera, theatre, dance, and film.

At the beginning of the Eighties, the shining stars in this firmament were John Lennon and Yoko Ono, who had apartments overlooking the park in the Dakota, 1 West 72nd Street, built for the upper middle class in 1884, the first grand luxury apartment house on the Upper West Side. At the entrance to the building on the night of 8 December 1980, John Lennon, 40, was gunned down by a madman. He was dead by the time he was rushed to Roosevelt Hospital. The official moment of death was recorded as 11.15pm. A tribute in memory of her late husband was the $1 million restoration by Yoko Ono Lennon, who continues to live in the Dakota, of Strawberry Fields, a tear-shaped, 3-acre section of the park in which the couple both loved to walk.

Elizabeth ("Betsy") Barlow Rogers took office in 1980 as Central Park Administrator, determined to arrest the years of neglect, evidenced here in the wrecked flat-bottomed boat and graffitied rock beside the Lake. The Central Park Conservancy, which she founded in 1985, has been the leading force in restoring what one writer called "that inimitable grass-and-granite drama that is Olmsted's artistic legacy ... The twin prongs of the Rogers strategy – intense restoration followed by vigilant maintenance – require vigorous enforcement. This is bound to create new conflicts with those conditioned by decades of anything-goes, who see their freedoms shrinking" (Tony Hendra, "Turf War," *New York*, 18 May 1998).

Betsy, a friend of the photographer, invited him to contribute to a dual photographic exhibition, "Ruth Orkin/Michael George: Two Perspectives of Central Park," sponsored by the Central Park Conservancy, 12 July-12 September 1983, in the Great Hall of the Dairy, the Gothic Revival building, beautifully restored, that was originally built to provide milk for nursing mothers in the park. In 1873, there were cows grazing on the meadows in front of the Dairy.

[115] – "Kiss My Cookies," a coffee shop, Christopher Street, between Bleecker and Hudson streets, Greenwich Village, Downtown Manhattan.

[116–117] – A party for TRH Prince and Princess Michael of Kent, Mortimer's, 1057 Lexington Avenue, at 75th Street, Upper East Side, Upper Manhattan, 26 October 1986.

An evening at which local movers and shakers had face time with visiting British minor royals, the Kents, was organised by the super-social, Athens-born, New York investment banker Alexander ("Alecko") P. Papamarkou (1930-98). Mortimer's, opened by Glenn Bernbaum in March 1976, on its twelfth anniversary in 1988, was described as "a neighbourhood restaurant carried to the most global extreme ... No one comes to Mortimer's just for the food ... tables of thin women who thoughtfully raise each shoestring potato to their mouths as though it requires a decision ... they will eat something like the chef's salad, which they can push around and pick at for hours, or the chicken paillard with the pat of herb butter on the top, which the women scrape off like it's a religious rite" (Julie Baumgold, "Inside Mortimer's, The High Life," "How We Live Now," *New York*, 20th Anniversary Special Issue III, 18 April 1988).

(*left*) HRH Princess Michael of Kent (1945-).

Wife of Prince Michael of Kent, she was born Baroness Marie-Christine von Reibnitz, in Bohemia, on the estate of her Austrian grandmother Princess Hedwig Windisch-Grätz, only daughter of Baron Günther von Reibnitz, an officer in the German army, by his wife, Countess Maria Szapáry. In 1971 she married Tom Troubridge, the merchant banker son of Vice-Admiral Sir Thomas Troubridge. In April 1978 she succeeded in having the marriage annulled; three months later she married Prince Michael of Kent in Vienna.

"She [Queen Elizabeth] was far from overjoyed by the prospect of the marriage and would have preferred a less exotic bride … Despite her looks, chic, and the powerful charm which she could exert, the glamour which she brought to the royal family was not appreciated nor regarded as a plus in public relations terms. The inner circle royal family saw her as an adventuress and her behaviour seemed to confirm their suspicions … referred to as 'Princess Pushy', 'the Valkyrie' and 'You Know Who' … The final embarrassment came with the revelation in 1985 that Marie-Christine's father, Baron von Reibnitz, had been a member of the SS …" (Sarah Bradford, *Elizabeth: A Biography of Her Majesty The Queen*, 1996).

(*right*) HRH Prince Michael of Kent (1942-).

Younger son of Prince George, Duke of Kent, and Princess Marina, Duchess of Kent, Prince Michael is a grandson of King George V, to whom he bears a striking resemblance. Although a minor royal, he had to obtain the consent of HM Queen Elizabeth II, his cousin, and renounce his position in the royal line of succession (sixteenth), before he could marry the former Mrs Tom Troubridge, the German-born Marie-Christine von Reibnitz, a Roman Catholic.

"Since his marriage, Prince Michael has concealed his dark good looks behind a greying beard that gives him an eerie resemblance to his distant cousin, the Tsar Nicholas II. Like his uncle the Duke of Windsor, he may also be identified by the excessive size of the knot in his tie. He and his family live in a grace-and-favour apartment in Kensington Palace …" (Kenneth Rose, *Kings, Queens & Courtiers/Intimate Portraits of the Royal House of Windsor from its foundation to the present day*, 1985).

[118] – A party for TRH Prince and Princess Michael of Kent, Mortimer's Restaurant, Lexington Avenue, Upper East Side, 26 October 1986.

(*above*) Mrs Estée Lauder. As she tells in her remarkable autobiography, *Estée: A Success Story*, America's most famous self-made woman, born Esther Mentzer, in Corona, Queens, started her own cosmetics business in the 1940s, and, with the help of her family, grew the company from a $800,000 cottage industry into a global brand with an annual turnover of $1.2 billion, and became the reigning beauty products queen.

(*below*) Mrs A. Alfred (Judy) Taubman. Among the favoured few gathered to meet the Kents, against the fabled bare brick of Mortimer's, was former Miss Israel Judy Mazor, the wife of Alfred Taubman, "a big, brutish man who made $800 million on strip shopping centers and malls and now owns most of Sotheby's" (Nell Scovell, "How to Marry a Millionaire," headlined "Golddiggers of 1987," *Spy*, September 1987).

After the Japanese had withdrawn from the international art market, and profits were down, Alfred Taubman got caught up in the long-running price-fixing scandal of Sotheby's and Christie's, the world's largest art auction houses. In 2001, despite his entering a plea of innocence, Taubman was found guilty by a federal jury, convicted, sentenced to a one-year jail term and ordered to pay a fine of $7.5 million. Forced to step down as chairman, he remained Sotheby's controlling shareholder. Without his personal contribution of $186 million, the fine imposed in a separate civil suit, which represented roughly five years of profits, could have bankrupted the company. The civil suit – a class action brought by customers of the two houses – was settled when Sotheby's and Christie's agreed to each pay $256 million to the plaintiffs.

[119] – A party to honour Ashton Hawkins, Executive Vice President and Counsel to the Trustees, The Metropolitan Museum of Art, Green Street, SoHo, Downtown Manhattan. May 1987.

(*above*) Lally Weymouth, neo-right-wing commentator and daughter of Katharine (Kay) Graham, *Washington Post* chairman, and Oscar de la Renta, irresistible Santo Domingo-born, New York fashion designer, and chairman, Queen Sofía Spanish Institute, 684 Park Avenue – location of the launch, 5 December 1993, of *The Gardens of Spain*, photographs by Michael George, text by Consuelo Martinez Correcher, published by Harry N. Abrams, Inc.

(*below*) Mrs Vincent (Brooke) Astor, and celebrity photographer Richard Avedon (1923-2004), who once said: "Sometimes I think all my pictures are just pictures of me."

[120–125] – Junior parties burgeoned in the late 1980s. This party, for up and coming New Yorkers, was given by the super-social, Athens-born, New York investment banker Alexander ("Alecko") P. Papamarkou (1930-98), at Jim McMullen's Restaurant, 1341 Third Avenue, Upper East Side, Uptown Manhattan, 27 March 1987.

[126] – The make-up artist to Lauren Bacall, Hollywood legend, making a triumphant return to the Broadway stage, in the city that, famously, never sleeps. The star's dressing room, Theater District, Midtown Manhattan.

[127] – An agent, with a great Rolodex, works the phone, Midtown Manhattan. "I ♥ NY," Milton Glazer's design classic, was devised as part of the city's clean-up campaign of 1975.

[128] – Tony Neal, Far West Village, Downtown Manhattan, 1980.

[129] – Matthew Ledbetter, Washington Heights, Uptown Manhattan.

[130] – Sam Dobbs, apartment of the photographer, Far West Village, Downtown Manhattan.

[131] – Jay Jenkins, apartment of the photographer, Far West Village, Downtown Manhattan.

[132] – *The Indian Hunter* (detail), SW of the Mall, Central Park, Uptown Manhattan. Bronze group; granite pedestal. John Quincy Adams Ward (1830-1910), sculptor. 1869.

Ward enlarged *The Indian Hunter* from a statuette he made in 1860 as an apprentice in the studio of Henry Kirke Brown. For authenticity, he went West, sketching the Native Americans in their hunting activities. Returning to New York, he worked full-scale in clay from the studies he had made, based on close observation in the Dakotas. In 1864 he was sufficiently satisfied to have it cast in plaster and exhibited. The acclaim ensured enough funds to have it cast in bronze and placed in Central Park, earning $10,000 for its creator. Before its permanent placement, he was invited to exhibit the work at the Paris Exposition in 1867 and at the National Academy of Design. The first piece of American sculpture to be placed in the 11-year-old Central Park, and Ward's first major commission, it established him as one of the leading post-Civil War sculptors.

[133] – Jay Jenkins, apartment of the photographer, Far West Village, Downtown Manhattan.

[135] – Gay Pride, Christopher Street, between Weehawken and West streets, Far West Village, Downtown Manhattan.

The Stonewall Riot which erupted on Christopher Street, 28 June 1969, was commemorated on the first anniversary in 1970 with the first gay liberation march, which swept through the Village. The event has since gone global as Pride Day.

> "I am a camera with its shutter open, quite passive, recording, not thinking … Some day, all this will have to be developed, carefully printed, fixed."
>
> Christopher Isherwood, "A Berlin Diary," *Goodbye to Berlin*, 1939

[136] – Pride-goers embrace on the route of the march, Midtown Manhattan.

[137] – "WE ARE FAMILY." LGBT community members and supporters parade in the city, Midtown Manhattan.

[138] – A power-dressing activist, Christopher Street, between Bleecker and Hudson streets, Greenwich Village, Downtown Manhattan.

[139] – "NATIONAL GAY TASK FORCE." Christopher Street, between Bleecker and Hudson streets, Greenwich Village, Downtown Manhattan.

[140–141] – The post-Pride scene, Far West Village, Downtown Manhattan.

(*left*) Messaging with a T-shirt, with two of New York's finest looking on, outside Badlands, a louche drinking den, West Street, NW corner Christopher Street.

(*right*) A crowd gathers on the waterfront at the foot of Christopher Street.

[142] – (*above*) Mirra Bank Brockman, West Broadway, SoHo, Downtown Manhattan. Film-maker. *Anonymous Was a Woman* was her first film.

(*below*) Marya Dalrymple, apartment of the photographer, Far West Village, Downtown Manhattan. A colleague at Harry N. Abrams, Inc., subsequently, as editor at Stewart, Tabori and Chang, Marya invited the photographer to contribute to the US edition of *Dumont Guide Ireland* (1981).

[143] – Martha Saxton, West 29th Street. Author of *Louisa May Alcott*, winner of the *Boston Globe* Annual Award in 1977, Secretary of PEN Executive Board 1986-89, co-founder in 2008 of *The Journal of the History of Childhood and Youth*, and, currently, Professor of History and Sexuality, Women's and Gender Studies and Elizabeth W. Bruss Reader, Amherst College, Massachusetts.

A friend and colleague in New York book publishing of the photographer (they first met in Paris in the 1960s), Martha was married to Enrico Ferorelli, the Italian-born photojournalist, for whom the photographer posed in his studio in January 1978.

[144–145] – Far West Village, Downtown Manhattan.

(*left, above*) Church of St Luke-in-the-Fields, Hudson Street, at the foot of Grove Street. John Heath or James N. Wells, architect. 1821-22.

and

Federal Archives Building, 645 Washington Street, between Christopher and Barrow streets. William J. Edbrooke, architect. 1899.

The severe, Federal-style church built of yellow brick, with an effective square tower, was photographed before the rebuilding necessitated by a devastating fire in 1980. Clement Clark Moore (1799-1863), compiler of the first Hebrew and Greek lexicons published in the United States, best remembered as the author of the perennially popular poem, "A Visit from St Nicholas" ("'Twas the Night Before Christmas"), was the first warden of St Luke's Episcopal Chapel, opened in 1822, on land that was part of Trinity Church farm. By contrast, the Federal Archives Building looming behind St Luke's, a massive, 10-storey, red-brick, Romanesque-Revival building, is considered New York's best piece of nineteenth-century industrial brickwork. It originally served as the Customs Appraisers warehouse, then functioned as the local Post Office and as a storage-house for records from the National Archives, before undergoing conversion to residential use in the 1980s.

(*left, below*) A lone reader, Hudson River pier building (since demolished) with, *right*, the block-square Federal Archives Building, Far West Village, Downtown Manhattan.

(*right, above*) Grove Court (detail), Grove Street, between Bedford and Hudson streets, Greenwich Village, Downtown Manhattan.

In Greenwich Village Historic District, designated 29 April 1969, lies Grove Court, one of the most delightfully secluded spots to be found anywhere on Manhattan Island. An ancient iron gateway gives admittance to only the boldest of spirits prepared to venture into one of the most exclusive addresses in New York: a red-brick-paved courtyard, shaded by trees, enclosing a group of six, white-shuttered, red-brick-fronted Federal houses, originally built for working men in the 1850s by Samuel Cocks, an enterprising grocer, who reckoned that having residents in the empty passage between No. 10 and No. 12 would help his business at No. 18 Grove Street.

(*right, below*) Hudson Street, west side, between West 10th and Charles streets, Far West Village, Downtown Manhattan.

In the unforgiving climate of New York, a break in the weather is welcomed by residents with a flurry of activity. The photographer lived at 525 Hudson Street, next door to the Post Office, in the second-floor apartment, with white-painted shutters, directly above Panache Vintage Clothing. Two years before he moved here in the summer of 1974, the Hudson Towers Tenants Association held a victory party presaging the end of one of the longest rent-strikes in New York City history. As reported by Charles Rose in *The Villager*, 15 June 1972, under the headline, "Hudson Towers Victory Ends 18-month Strike,"

> "The celebration was for a collective bargaining contract signed May 18 between the H.T.T.A. and the landlord, 519 Hudson Realty Corp., which could result in $47,000 of major repairs and capital improvements for the five association buildings at 255 and 257 W.10th St., and at 521, 523 and 525 Hudson Street. At the block party tenants talked about their long fight. For the last five years there were no front door locks on any of the buildings, tenant Rick Rossein said. 'Tenants were victims of gun-point robberies and attempted rapes, as well as drug addicts prowling the halls.' He said some apartments were burglarized several times in the same day. Four months ago, tenants installed two front door locks on the buildings at 521 and 255; they painted their own hallways. 'It seemed we had to do everything, even the heating was poor,' Rossein added …"

Two blocks north on Hudson Street lived Jane Jacobs, writer and urban activist. In *The Death and Life of Great American Cities*, published in 1961 and now recognised as a classic work, she wrote:

> "Under the seeming disorder of the old city, wherever the old city is working successfully, is a marvellous order for maintaining the safety of the streets. It is a complex order: its essence is intricacy of pavement use, bringing with it a constant succession of eyes. The order is all composed of movement and change, and although it is life, not art, we may fancifully call it the art form of the city and liken it to the dance."

[146–147] – Far West Village.

A party hosted by Revd and Mrs Ledlie Laughlin, St Luke's Vicarage, Hudson Street, between Christopher and Barrow streets, Far West Village, Downtown Manhattan. The red-brick vicarage, built just south of the church in 1823, is the oldest, in continuing use, in the city.

(*left*) Revd James Harold Flye (1884-1985), Episcopal priest (ordained in 1915), teacher, poet, and photographer, is quietly absorbed in reading. For thirty-six years Father Flye was at St Andrew's School in Sewanee, Tennessee, where he taught history, among other subjects. In 1919, the year following his arrival, he first met James Agee, Rufus Agee, as he was called then, a boy just under ten years of age, who had recently lost the father whom, much later, he described in his novel *A Death in the Family*, published posthumously in 1957. Best remembered as the mentor and confidant of the co-author, with photographer Walker Evans, of *Let Us Now Praise Famous Men* (1941), Father Flye was responsible for publishing, in 1962, *Letters of James Agee to Father Flye*, a moving record of the thirty-five years of friendship between the two men. In the early 1980s the photographer got to know, and photograph, his near neighbour Father Flye, whom he visited, often in the company of Harvey Simmonds, another St Luke's resident, in the room in the parish house, filled with books and memorabilia, including cartons of ribbon-bound letters, he had occupied since his retirement in 1959. In a letter to James Agee, dated 8 May 1943, Father Flye wrote:

> "Why should one long so to preserve in permanent form thoughts, records of incidents, photographs? This seems based on a deep-lying assumption that one's own life will continue or that there will be others in the future to whom such things will mean something of what they mean to oneself. There will be such persons, no doubt, but how many? and the chance of getting into the possession of such persons the things one values and preserves – to say nothing of many successions of such handing on – seems small. Much of what Mrs Flye or you or I would treasure would to many people be just rubbish, to be burned up in house-cleaning. One cannot reach out his hand beyond his own lifetime to put into the hand of another who would really care for them, things which he has felt worth preserving – if they can be kept even as long as he himself lives."

Among the photographer's treasured possessions is a copy of the *Letters*, inscribed by Father Flye, St David's Day, 1982.

(*right, above*) Sally Fisher and Erik Wensberg, poets.

(*right, below*) Harvey (Brother Benedict) Simmonds (1938-2013).

A person of great gifts, the greatest of which was of friendship, the self-effacing, mild-mannered, kind Harvey Simmonds was, variously, planting and caring for the Native Plant Garden of the New York Botanical Garden; studying at Columbia "towards rare book and manuscript librarianship"; a member of the staffs of the Manuscript Division, Berg Collection, and Editor's Office of the New York Public Library; Librarian of the Grolier Club,

America's oldest bibliophile club; Director of the Eakins Press, founded by his friend Leslie George Katz; and, in a break from New York, working on the steamboat *Delta Queen*, on which he experienced, in his own words, "the agitated pleasures of paddlewheel living."

As a newly arrived member of the staff of the Editorial Office of the New York Public Library in 1971, Harvey Simmonds was asked to prepare for printing the text of an exhibition for the Library for the Performing Arts at Lincoln Center. The text was by Lincoln Kirstein. Later, at the Eakins Press, of which Lincoln Kirstein was "a full partner," Harvey Simmonds was to enjoy a productive working relationship with Kirstein, president of the School of American Ballet (which he founded, with George Balanchine, in 1934), general director of the New York City Ballet (which both men founded in 1948), and "whose ubiquitous midwifery is traceable through so much that is fine and indispensable in twentieth-century American culture" (Lloyd Fonvielle, Essay, *Walker Evans*, Masters of Photography, 1979).

At Williams College in Massachusetts, Harvey Simmonds often hitchhiked to watch ballet from the gods, then sleep at Grand Central Station. At Eakins Press, Harvey Simmonds' early appreciation of classical ballet was to be channelled into researching, over a five-year period, the work of Balanchine for the first catalogue raisonné devoted to a choreographer. In a preface to *Choreography by George Balanchine*, Eakins Press, 1983, Lincoln Kirstein wrote:

> "The essence of ballet … is order … There has undoubtedly occurred what must be called an unfocused but active revival of religious interest in the West, seeking unfamiliar access to an absolute. It is not too much to consider a well-performed ballet a rite, executed and followed with intense devotion, that shares in some sort of moral figuration. The response of the audience to good dancing is a release of body and breath, a thanksgiving that is selfless, generous, complete, and leaves the spectator corroborated in the hope that despite the world and its horrors, here somehow is a paradigm of perfection."

If Harvey Simmonds was "seeking unfamiliar access to an absolute," he was to find it, perhaps, at Holy Cross Abbey, Berryville, Virginia, which he entered, having made his profession to Cistercian monastic life, in the same year, 1983, in which *Choreography by George Balanchine*, arguably his greatest achievement as editor, was published. "That concentration of focused intelligence free of self-vaunting," attributed to his friend and colleague Leslie Katz, but which was, pre-eminently, in Harvey's gift, in those years at the Eakins Press in which, as he wrote, "I knew something of the struggle toward textual precision," submitted, finally, to the "sixth-century Rule of Saint Benedict as it has been lived in the Cistercian tradition since the eleventh century" (*Conversatio: Cistercian Monastic Life*, A Limited-Edition Portfolio. Photographs by Lance Hidy. Text by Carolyn Coman. Edited by Brother Benedict Simmonds).

In *The Butterfly Garden* (2010), the book of colour photographs by Beverly Pearce of the garden that he had planned and planted, Brother Benedict Simmonds wrote, "My earliest memory is of a flower – of my mother holding me up before the lowest branch of a Royal Poinciana tree in the garden of the house my father built for her in Cape Mount, Liberia." Harvey Simmonds was born in Liberia in 1938 to Episcopal missionary parents who built a school at Cape Mount. After the war, the family, which now included Harvey's younger brother Andrew, settled in Sewanee, Tennessee. The boys' priest and history teacher at St Andrew's School was Father James Harold Flye, who mentored James Agee. Many years later, when both men were leading members of the close-knit community of St Luke's on Hudson Street (and the photographer was their near neighbour and friend), Harvey put together *Through the Eyes of A Teacher/ Photographs by Father James Harold Flye*, edited by Donald Dietz and David Herwaldt, with a foreword by Robert Coles, 1980.

In 1999 Brother Benedict was diagnosed with kidney disease and in 2005 he was advised that he had only months to live. He survived another seven years.

> "To coordinate is to create. For example, when Harvey Simmonds (Brother Benedict) was chosen to lead the magnificent task of assembling a complete, detailed listing of every ballet George Balanchine devised during his protean career, everyone who knew him had complete confidence in his ability. In the process the staff he led found themselves in touch with the Universe. The entire world is Harvey's community and connecting it is his mission."

> Leslie George Katz

[148] – Interior, apartment of the photographer. 15 January 1983.

The antique American rocking chair was the first item of furniture purchased by the photographer following his move from a fifth-floor walk-up on the Lower East Side to a railroad apartment in the Far West Village in the summer of 1974. On the wall behind are a *pichwai*, an Indian painting on cloth, a souvenir of his travels with friends in the subcontinent in October 1976, and "*Oscar,*" a caricature of Oscar Wilde by "Ape" (Carlo Pellegrini), *Vanity Fair*, 24 May 1884, purchased in London, where he worked in the book trade from 1965 to 1971. This image, and its companion piece opposite, were taken to mark the photographer's fortieth birthday.

> "But even in this chamber there was a rocking chair. It would be impossible to get anywhere in America, without a rocking chair."

> Charles Dickens, *American Notes for General Circulation*, 1842

[149] – Michael George, self-portrait. 15 January 1983.

> "Everything is autobiographical and everything is a portrait."

> Lucian Freud

"This is the best of me ... this I saw and knew: this, if anything of mine, is worth your memory."

John Ruskin, *Sesame and the Lilies*, 1865